HOLLOWING OUT THE MIDDLE

Hollowing Out the Middle

The Rural Brain Drain and
What It Means for America

Patrick J. Carr and
Maria J. Kefalas

Beacon Press
BOSTON

BEACON PRESS
25 Beacon Street
Boston, Massachusetts 02108-2892
www.beacon.org

Beacon Press books
are published under the auspices of
the Unitarian Universalist Association of Congregations.

12   11   10   09   8   7   6   5   4   3   2   1

This book is printed on acid-free paper that meets the uncoated paper
ANSI/NISO specifications for permanence as revised in 1992.

Text design and composition by Wilsted and Taylor Publishing Services

Maps were designed by Jonathan Dart.

Library of Congress Cataloging-in-Publication Data

Carr, Patrick J.
    Hollowing out the middle : the rural brain drain and what it means for
America / Patrick J. Carr, Maria J. Kefalas.
        p. cm.
    Includes bibliographical references and index.
    ISBN 978-0-8070-4238-0 (hardcover : alk. paper)
    1. Cities and towns—United States—History—21st century. 2. Cities
and towns—Growth—History—21st century. 3. Youth—United
States—Social life and customs—21st century. I. Kefalas, Maria.
II. Title.
    HT123.C387 2009
    307.760973'0905—dc22   2009010392

Dedicated to the memory of
Katy Hennessey (1968–1991)

CONTENTS

Preface

W HY SHOULD WE CARE ABOUT THE future of small towns
in the Heartland? If many of them disappear and become
latter-day ghost towns, what real difference will it make to most
of our lives? Though the small town claims an iconic place in the
American psyche, we are considerably less alarmed by the emptying
out of prairie and plains towns than by the endangered status of the
polar bear, an altogether more universally vulnerable symbol and
one that our kids can easily comprehend and mourn the loss of. You
don't need to be a coastal elitist or a laissez-faire apologist to make
the case that the hollowing out of the Heartland is an inevitable result of boom-and-bust cycles that, by their very nature, must have
winners and losers. And there is more than a grain of truth to such
an analysis in that many mining or frontier towns have ceased to
exist over the years as their fortunes have waned. But this time it
is different. The hollowing out that we describe here is more widespread, debilitating, and, we will contend, ultimately detrimental
not only to the region but to the nation as a whole. What is happening in many small towns—the devastating loss of educated and
talented young people, the aging of the population, and the erosion
of the local economy—has repercussions far beyond their bound-

aries. Put simply, the health of the small towns that are dotted across the Heartland matters because, without them, the country couldn't function, in the same way that a body cannot function without a heart.

As we neared completion of this book, almost seven years after we first began, we were asked to show more explicitly why hollowing out mattered. Because we are, first and foremost, researchers, we put this same question to several people whose roots in the Midwest run deep. Their responses varied from apoplexy to bewilderment that we should even ask. "Of course it matters," they chorused, and, in their separate ways, they went on to say why small towns are worth saving. One person talked about how much of the nation's natural resources and the world's food comes from this region and said that this alone should be incentive to devote attention to the challenges facing the countryside. Another pointed out that if alternative forms of energy and food production are the waves of the future, then the Midwest and rural areas more generally will be ground zero for the rolling out of the green economy and sustainable agriculture. A third alluded to the historical centrality of the region to the health of the nation and said that, despite the recent downturn in manufacturing and the wholesale reordering of agriculture, the Heartland and its thousands of towns could, with the right policies in place, once again thrum with success. And a fourth said that not caring about the rural crisis was akin to saying that the North should have let the South secede in the mid-nineteenth century; America is strongest when it is unified.

As we digested the assorted responses to the question of why we should care about small-town America, we instinctively knew that they contained some basic truths about the challenges that rural America faces. We had seen firsthand the herculean efforts that some small towns make to survive and the ferocious love that inhabitants feel for their dot on the map. And yet it was in the younger generation's stories about coming-of-age in the Heartland that the most important lessons about the workings of small towns were revealed. The time we spent living in Iowa brought home to us the fragility of places that on the surface appear prosperous. One patch of bad luck—a shuttered factory or the realization that there aren't enough children to keep a local school open—can bring a community to its knees. We came to learn how the precarious existence of the northeastern Iowa town we would get to know so intimately was mirrored in hundreds of other places throughout the nation. We also found that because of the slow and insidious nature of this threat, the rural downturn is happening in what amounts to splendid isolation.

We are not experts on rural America, small towns, or regional development. In fact, in our combined professional lives, we have spent all our time and spilled all our ink on urban issues and problems. But as converts are often identifiable by the strength of their zeal, our immersion in this issue fueled a great desire to place the hollowing-out phenomenon on the crowded national to-do list. We do so because we believe that there are more than quaint postcard images of sepia-toned Main Streets at stake. We should care because the Heartland is the place where our food comes from, it is the place that helps elect our presidents—who would doubt the centrality of winning in Iowa for Barack Obama's campaign?—and it is the place that sends more than its fair share of young men and women to fight for this country. The future of the many towns that give the Heartland its shape and its sinews is of vital importance, and we believe that ignoring their hollowing out will be detrimental in the short and long terms. Though we are faced with an economic crisis of ever-widening and catastrophic proportions that will undoubtedly siphon our attention and resources, it would be a mistake to overlook the crisis in rural America that has slowly developed over the past two decades. In many ways the travails of hollowing out small towns and their Main Streets were an ominous harbinger of economic hard times to come. It is unfortunate that so few people were paying attention that the warning slipped by unheeded.

To be fair, we should say at the outset that when we started our research we had no real idea that we would be talking about the future of small towns. As with most projects there was a great deal of serendipity involved, and we initially intended to examine only the experiences of young adults from nonmetropolitan America. That we should be even doing this is ascribable to the vision of Frank Furstenberg and the largesse of the MacArthur Foundation. In the fall of 2001, the Research Network on Transitions to Adulthood, headed by Furstenberg and supported by the foundation, embarked upon a project to interview young adults in several different locations in the country. The group had already settled on the coastal bookends of New York City and San Diego, and Midwest metropolitan and suburban sites in the Minneapolis/St. Paul and Greater Detroit areas. But Furstenberg felt that something was missing from this plan, and so we were summoned to a meeting at the Russell Sage Foundation in New York City, where he and several senior colleagues outlined to us their vague wish list for a fifth site. They wanted us to find a place that was "small, you know, like a small town with one school" and that was "in the middle somewhere" and "far away from a big city and the ocean" and "in one of those red states." There was some talk of wanting the site to be in the Bible Belt and of having us work in two different places, but that was quickly quashed, and we were given the lunch break to consider how we might meet the aspirations of Furstenberg's organization and where the ideal place for the research might be. Though at least one of the senior scholars at this meeting was visibly aghast that a pair of greenhorns should be entrusted with developing a research site, as we talked things over at lunch we felt that we could do the job and that we knew a town that could be the perfect site. Pat had first visited Ellis* when he was traveling through America in 1989. He had become friends with a native who had been on a summer exchange program in Dublin, and, as the town fit the parameters of small, nonmetropolitan, and in the middle, we were sure that it could be just the place. After our meal we were asked to point out "where this Ellis is" on the map. The response was positive. We were soon dispatched to interview young adults who had attended Ellis High School in the late 1980s and early 1990s about their transition to adulthood and to see how it compared with that of their peers on the coasts and in the cities and suburbs of the Midwest.

The research network had decided to do what columnist David Brooks was soon to advocate in an article called "One Nation, Slightly Divisible," in which he famously described the cultural divide between coastal America and Middle America. Though Brooks falls into exaggerated characterizations and stereotypes of his own, he does so to make the larger point that we know very little about "Red America as seen through Red America's eyes."[1] The Heartland Project, as the Iowa research was dubbed, was a first step toward just that kind of understanding, and we were surprised at the path that the project came to take.

During the first interviews with these young Iowans originally from Ellis, we stumbled upon the key event that helped us to understand not only their individual trajectories but also the waxing and waning fortunes of their hometown. As they explained to us, the biggest question facing anyone who grows up in a small town is whether he or she should leave or stay. A little further down the road, those who make the initial decision to leave, usually after

---

*Ellis is a pseudonym. The convention in ethnographic research is to protect the community and its residents' privacy. So, though the quotes and stories we share are absolutely true, some minor details and names have been changed to guarantee confidentiality.

graduating high school, must decide whether to return to the cozy familiarity of their hometown or to continue building lives elsewhere. The fact that this small-town rite of passage should be so intimately bound up with the very future of the Heartland allows us to see how the hollowing-out phenomenon plays out in the lives and decisions of young people, and how their pathways are shaped by the communities and people who surround them as they grow up. Though socioeconomic cycles affect the conditions that shape these places and expand or constrict the options available to small towns, it is people's actions that ultimately determine whether a place hollows out. In what follows, we give voice to this process through the words and experiences of young people from a typical small town in rural Iowa. We do so because, in the end, we can come to know this problem only through these testimonies, and they allow us to comprehend what can be lost if hollowing out is not addressed. We believe that saving small-town America ought to be a priority, and in the pages that follow we show how it might be done.

The Heartland and the Rural Youth Exodus

For generations in our national life, progress was the preserve of cities. . . . Inventions, standards of services, and social styles and trends lagged in their adoption in rural areas. The countryside was a time machine in which urbanites could see the living past, and feel nostalgic or superior, as the sight inclined them. —Calvin Beale

I N A FAST-PACED AND UNCERTAIN WORLD, it is comforting to believe in small-town America's idyllic possibilities. The trouble is that few people ever seem to penetrate much deeper than the bucolic ideal. A closer and more clear-eyed examination reveals that our country is in the throes of a most painful and unpredictable transition. In what has become an all-too-familiar story, rural states such as North Dakota and West Virginia share an unsettling problem: too many young people in their twenties and thirties are leaving. Rural counties in Kansas and Georgia report the highest rates of population loss nationally, and this hemorrhaging of people, specifically the younger generation, is hollowing out many of the nation's small towns and rural communities. The rural youth exodus is not a new phenomenon; young people have always left small towns for big cities and bright opportunities. But as the new century's first decade ends, the loss of such a huge share of them could spell the end of small-town America.

Headlines from both the *New York Times* and *Los Angeles Times* blame rural out-migration on "regional competition" from "warmer climates and hipper scenes." This explanation suggests that the flight of young adults is a natural occurrence, an inevitable consequence of progress, and that there is little reason to worry. However, with time and taken altogether, these individual choices have devastating consequences for the communities left behind. Scattered throughout the nation, thousands of towns find themselves twenty, ten, or even five years away from extinction because there are too few taxpayers, consumers, and workers to keep going. For many locales, the final death knell sounds when there are no longer enough children to keep the doors of the area school open.

Economists warn that shifts in population among professional-class elites have contributed to uneven economic growth nationally. During the 1990s, the rise of Richard Florida's "creative class"[1]—educated and entrepreneurial cultural consumers and producers—and the infusions of human capital they brought with them injected cities such as Austin and Phoenix with a potent booster shot. "Left behind are those regional losers—the laggard, blue-collar red states"[2] that find themselves fighting to keep their communities and counties viable as the destructive social forces of graying populations and depopulation take their toll. During the past half-century, Iowa, North Dakota, and West Virginia ranked dead last—forty-eighth, forty-ninth, and fiftieth, respectively—among all the states for population growth.[3] This accompanying map shows the more than seven hundred rural counties that have lost 10 percent or more of their populations since 1980. The greatest outflow is on the plains, from North Dakota through Texas.

DECIMATION OF AMERICA'S HEARTLAND

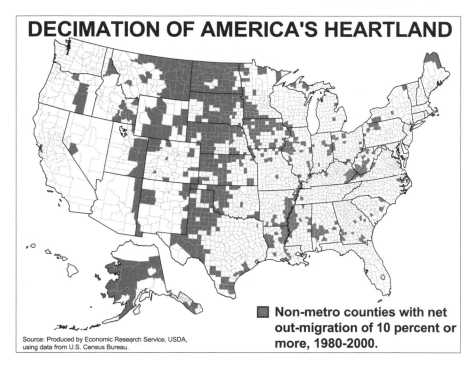

■ Non-metro counties with net out-migration of 10 percent or more, 1980-2000.

Source: Produced by Economic Research Service, USDA, using data from U.S. Census Bureau.

The decisions that young people on the edge of adulthood make about whether to stay or leave home have profound implications for the future of rural America. The fact is that the birth of a child cannot replace what small towns lose every time a young adult moves away. Because twenty-somethings are the ones leaving the countryside in such dramatic numbers, we might expect the stark realities of the economy and the more effervescent nature of being young to rank among the more obvious reasons for their concentration in metropolitan areas. No one would deny that finding work in today's countryside means facing a triple threat: a failing farm- and factory-based economy, rising unemployment, and shrinking wages and benefits. Contrary to conventional thinking about the "problem with young people today" who are bored with life in the countryside, the majority of young people who are leaving aren't motivated by the possibility of trading in flannel shirts and pickup trucks for Diesel jeans and club scenes. Leaving small-town life requires a plan and a willingness to cut oneself off from a world that is familiar and predictable. There are some young people who can't wait to break free, but far more choose the ties and obligations of home, where things just seem to get harder. They fear that the outside world will expect them to change too much of who and what they are.

The problem of rapidly aging demographics in nonmetropolitan[4] counties, a majority of which now have fewer residents under age eighteen than they did a decade ago and more deaths than births, is not our sole concern.[5] Another, perhaps more pressing problem is that the young people moving away include the most highly educated.[6] In a twenty-first-century world, acquiring human capital through education and training brings with it the promise of socioeconomic and geographic mobility, and so the flight of the countryside's young people is also a brain drain. Back in 1940, when just 5 percent of Americans possessed a college education, degreed teachers, physicians, and business owners were scattered across small towns and cities fairly evenly.[7] By 1970, five years after President Lyndon B. Johnson signed the Higher Education Act[8] into law, thus creating a massive, federally funded financial-aid system and dramatically expanding access to higher education for Americans from all walks of life, "only five percentage points separated the most highly educated regions in the United States from the least highly educated regions."[9] Three decades later, in 2000, "the regional educational gap" had more than *doubled* to 13 percentage points.[10] In New England, the most highly educated region of the United States, one-third of the adult residents possess bachelor's degrees, while in the southern section of the nation—in Alabama, Mississippi, Tennessee, and Kentucky—fewer than one in five adults could make the same claim.[11]

Although the brain-drain phenomenon does not afflict only the countryside—upstate New York and Philadelphia lose more educated people than they gain—the picture "is particularly bleak for rural America,"[12] where, in any given year, more than 6 percent of America's nonmetropolitan bachelor's degree–holders migrate to a metropolitan area.[13] One of the clearest symptoms of this problem is the fact that it is now a struggle to find replacements for retiring small-town doctors, business owners, and teachers in much of the countryside.[14] The youth exodus is a zero-sum phenomenon: it benefits the destination cities and hurts the regions that migrants flee. For every thriving metropolis now, there are dozens of agroindustrial brain-drain areas where economic growth has stalled. Experts believe these regions are in so much trouble largely because too few of their most-likely-to-succeed types with college credentials and upwardly mobile aspirations remain, and too many of the local kids with vocational certificates and the most diminished economic prospects do.[15]

AN OLD WAY OF LIFE COMES TO AN END

Throughout the twentieth century, generations of young people coming of age in the countryside depended on family farms or local plants for their livelihood. As the seismic shifts in agriculture and manufacturing made firms and farms outsource and automate, rural regions witnessed a collapsing demand for labor.[16] With fewer opportunities for work that paid a decent wage, more young people found it necessary to abandon this old way of life. Despite the emptying out of the Heartland and the myriad forces conspiring against rural areas' backbone industries, the nation's belief in the insulated vibrancy of small towns appears oddly unshaken. Yet look beyond the postcard-perfect barns standing empty and unused: they are the rural equivalent of the inner city's shuttered factories and crumbling smokestacks.[17] Although the fact that there are fewer farms in Iowa today is common knowledge, the extent of the financial and demographic devastation in agriculture is less well known: just 2 percent of Americans operate farms now, for example, and 42 percent of Midwestern farms earn less than $20,000 a year.[18] By the end of the twentieth century, independent farmers became "more like modern-day sharecroppers," and "the Jeffersonian ideal of pastoral life" was subsumed by "the corporate, agribusiness model of mega-farms."[19] The fundamental paradox of the family farm's demise—which kept the rest of us from seeing how bad things had become—was that the single greatest cause of the rural crisis was, more than anything else, progress.[20] Improvements in crop science and innovations in farm management boosted output while reducing the need for farmers themselves.[21] In the end, "the intrusion of technology"[22] into the countryside would become one of the single most important reasons for depopulation.

During the 1970s and '80s, when agriculture started going corporate and the credit crisis drove so many off their land, farmers looking for a new way to support themselves believed they had gotten a reprieve with the arrival of new manufacturing jobs. Grateful ex-farmers ignored how these companies and their competitors had fled cities and other towns in search of cheap labor and land. The farmers, who lost everything in places such as Iowa and Minnesota, just wanted to rebuild their lives and raise their kids. In the countryside, there was a long history of using nonfarm work to make up for lost incomes during those years with disappointing harvests, and many thought that building Deere tractors or Maytag washers would be the answer to their prayers. But just as they settled into work on an assembly line, they would hear rumors of layoffs or of relocation to another state—or maybe even to China or Mexico—where the local politicians promised the bosses even sweeter sweetheart deals. Harvard University sociologist William Julius Wilson famously chronicled how the very same processes of deindustrialization, unemployment, global market shifts, and the flight of the middle class gave rise to hyper-ghettoes and fueled the decline of cities.[23] As millions[24] of factory jobs left the countryside, the identical global market transformations behind the urban crisis gave rise to a rural one.

And just as in the inner cities, those left behind in shattered small towns have felt the consequences of this demographic shift in a host of social problems, among them rising rates of poverty. Of the twenty-five poorest counties in the nation, five are in Nebraska, and four are in Texas and South Dakota. Nebraska's Loup County has a per capita personal income of $6,404.[25] Nonmarital childbearing is on the rise in Iowa, where one in four first births is to an unmarried woman. And in Oklahoma, which has the dubious distinction of having the highest divorce rate in the nation, welfare dependency and poverty among women and children have overwhelmed state officials.[26] In addition, the rate of serious crime in Kansas and Nebraska in 2002, the peak of the methamphetamine epidemic, was as much as 50 percent higher than in the state of New York. In 2004, the Iowa Division of Narcotics Enforcement reported fifteen hundred meth-lab busts in the state, which was the second-highest number of any state in the nation, behind only Missouri. According to recent data from the U.S. Drug Enforcement Administration, that ranking has improved with the dramatic decline in meth labs. Still, in 2006, Iowa recorded the sixth-highest number of meth-lab incidents in the United States as a whole.[27]

When one economic phase ends and another begins, the negative effects are never felt equally by everyone, and this was no less true in the Heartland. At the moment that manufacturing declined and agriculture got supersized, other societal changes opened up opportunities for those ready to take advantage of them—specifically, greater access to higher education, particularly among women. What the new economy's winners grasped was that the hunger for highly skilled labor would mean college credentials were no longer a luxury but a necessity for those serious about assuring their place in the middle class. Young people have always left small towns to attend college, but by the early 1990s there were more opportunities and more compelling reasons to do so than ever before.

Even as getting a college degree became increasingly possible for greater numbers of high school graduates, it was the children of the middle and upper middle classes, not surprisingly, who were following this path in far greater numbers. And because the drive to leave had long been connected to earning a degree, in less than a generation the Heartland's most valuable export was no longer its crops or hogs but its educated young people.[28] As the highly skilled, highly educated, and highly paid congregated in superstar cities such as San Francisco and Boston, their counterparts of more modest means, educations, and resources were left behind in depopulating rural areas from the Great Plains to the Mississippi Delta.[29] These class-structured migration patterns reinforce a level of uneven development not seen since the Civil War.[30]

Given the scope of these changes and the fact that one in five Americans lives in nonmetropolitan areas, what is most surprising is that more attention has not been paid to the future of small towns. "The same politicians who decried the moral, economic, and social decline of cities," notes the writer Timothy Egan, "have been largely silent about the rural downturn."[31] One can speculate that since rural communities are sparsely populated, their problems are more often hidden from view. Perhaps the rural crisis has developed so slowly that the symptoms of decline have been easier to ignore; the rural downturn seeped rather than swept through the region.[32] But it is also quite possible that the main reason is denial; no one wants to admit that the small town's *Music Man* image is nothing more than cockeyed nostalgia.

Though demographers provide us with meticulously tabulated reports about how much the countryside has changed, the truth is that we know precious little about what's behind depopulation and what really motivates the young people driving out-migration. What we do know is that their decisions have undeniable consequences for huge sections of the nation. Talk to the experts, and there are two schools of thought about why young people leave small towns. Economists blame a shortage of jobs, while sociologists and geographers contend that there is a shortage of things to do.[33] What both explanations gloss over is why and how the young people leaving look so markedly different from the ones who don't.

Spend time in the middle of the nation, in one of the thousands of small towns where the hollowing-out process has taken hold, and you see a growing chasm between the people leaving and the ones who remain. Fueling the out-migration trends is a regional filtering system pushing some young people to stay and others to go. Leaving, or not, does not result only from young people's individual preferences; instead, it is a reflection of their resources, particularly the messages they receive from their social networks. Simply put, leaving is something that young people must be pushed, prodded, and cultivated to do, whereas staying just sort of happens. Given that young people are now rural America's most precious declining resource, it seems that the best way to preserve the nation's small towns will be to create new sorts of conservation efforts to invest more efficiently in these young people, whose futures—as parents, workers, homeowners, voters, and taxpayers—will be so critical to the countryside's survival.

LIVING IN ELLIS, IOWA

We moved to Iowa to try to understand the hollowing-out story. The state of Iowa provides a useful bellwether case: only West Virginia loses a larger percentage of its college graduates to out-migration, and because of this loss of young adults Iowa is aging more quickly than the rest of the nation. During the 1980s, the farm crisis dramatically reshaped agriculture in the state, long considered the buckle of the nation's Corn Belt.[34] Now, only seven other states are more dependent than Iowa on manufacturing in terms of gross domestic product.[35] In just three years, from 2000 to 2003, Iowa lost thirty thousand manufacturing jobs, more than 10 percent of the state's total. During the next five years, work crept back into the region, but the new jobs were inferior to the old ones, offering fewer benefits and lower wages. Some companies shifted operations overseas, while others, lured away by other regions' tax breaks, just crossed state lines. But in the one-plant towns where people depend on jobs at Maytag or Winnebago, persistent unemployment and shuttered businesses are the first signs that things will get worse before they get better.

On a more symbolic level, Iowa embodies a distinctive "middleness," a reassuring typicality in the national self-perception.[36] Everyone from presidential hopefuls to rock-star activists[37] visits the state when they want to take the nation's pulse on an issue. After all, Iowa is the Heartland, the place where the "real" and supposedly more authentic[38] Americans reside.

We chose, for our research, a town we call "Ellis," in the northeastern corner of the state, because it is typical of the many towns that are finding it difficult to survive, and its travails could be those of any of the thousands of depopulating rural communities stretching from western Pennsylvania to the Texas Panhandle. Ellis, with its population of 2,014, is not quite large enough to merit a streetlight, but there is a bank, two gas stations, and a family-run grocery store. Like most Iowa towns, regardless of their size, Ellis has two Lutheran churches (the conservative Missouri Synod and more liberal Reformed), and a Catholic, Methodist, and Evangelical church.

As Iowa towns go, Ellis is not noteworthy for its historical significance or its scenic beauty. With grain elevators, a John Deere dealership, and farms perched on the town's outskirts, Ellis has the "look and feel of a farming community with its roots deep in the land."[39] One must remember, though, that Iowa's farm communities are not exactly what they seem, since few people still depend solely on the land for their livelihood.[40] Indeed, the most conspicuous aspects of the town's landscape may be the very things that are missing: malls, subdivisions, traffic, and young people. In this day and age, when so many people live in communities that look identical, Ellis is fifteen miles away from the nearest McDonald's, forty miles away from the closest Wal-Mart, and, while we lived there, nearly eighty miles from a Starbucks. And the town's graying population means that the median age is forty-four, nearly a decade older than the nation as a whole. Ellis's aging demographics are common throughout the rural Midwest, where the average median age in nonmetropolitan counties now approaches thirty-nine: in fact, nearly 40 percent of the Midwest's nonmetropolitan counties have median ages older than forty years, whereas less than 1 percent of the Midwest metropolitan counties do.[41]

The young people who came of age in Ellis in the late 1980s and early 1990s made their transition to adulthood at a critical juncture for rural America. During the three decades of their lives so far, one in three of Iowa's farms disappeared, the percentage of Americans with college degrees increased by one-third, and the Heartland states of Iowa, Kansas, Nebraska, and the Dakotas lost hundreds of thousands of factory jobs. During the 1980s, when they attended grade school, the credit crisis pushed family farmers over the cliff. By the time they were in high school, in the early 1990s, the high-tech economy was coming to prominence: their decisions to stay, leave, or return would help seal the fate of the entire region.

In 2002, we moved our family to Ellis[42] and crisscrossed the nation—from California to Florida and New Mexico to Massachu-setts[43]—during a span of eighteen months to speak with young people who had attended Ellis High School.[44] This was not the first time we had joined a community to write a book about a place and its people, but our preferred modus operandi is to fade into the background as much as possible. You might assume that two college professors hanging out on corners talking with teen mothers and drug dealers in Philadelphia's Badlands might stand out, but in Philly, most passersby assumed we were caseworkers or cops, frequent visitors to the city's toughest and most troubled neighborhoods. But the minute we arrived in Ellis, we came to be known as the folks renting Libby Duncan's house, and our presence garnered far more attention than we expected or might have liked. Most people made no effort to mask their polite, yet intense, curiosity about what the professors from back East were doing there. Soon after we moved to town, our arrival was heralded in a story in the *Ellis Gazette*. The newspaper's owner, editor-in-chief, primary reporter, and oc-casional photographer requested an interview with us. Assuming that the piece would be hidden away behind the graduation notices and the want ads, we agreed. A few days later, the front-page lead story, with an above-the-fold headline, announced that the town had been selected to be part of a "national study." Not long afterward, a television reporter from Cedar Rapids and a newspaper columnist from Waterloo called. They wanted to do their own stories on the Heartland Project, us, and what we were studying about Ellis. On both those occasions, we declined, as we had learned our lesson.

We were not celebrities, but it was as though the circus had come to town, and we were one of the main acts. Neither of us is from Iowa, and, though we had lived in Chicago for years, we had only driven through towns like Ellis on our way to someplace else. In places like Ellis, where people stay put for generations, there is a constant accounting of arrivals and departures. Outsiders get tagged and classified through their connections, no matter how attenuated, to the long-term inhabitants. For instance, the owner of one of Ellis's businesses, though he has been in town for more than a decade, is still known as the fellow who moved into Dr. Stillworth's house. For us, our tie was through Dennis and Laura Daugherty. Mentioning them did not always help open doors, but often it did ease suspicions. Pat had met the family when their middle daughter, Kelly, studied in Ireland a decade earlier. We realized quickly that the Daugherty family name almost always granted us safe passage. The first time we tried by phone to set up a meeting with a local minister, he did everything to avoid us except hang up on us. The moment we mentioned that Dennis and Laura had suggested we call, his cool politeness thawed into warm enthusiasm. "Why didn't you say so in the first place?" he would ask later.

This wariness about new people and the desire to maintain the routines of small-town life reflect that one of the greatest pleasures of such an existence is being surrounded by people you know, people who share similar expectations about what constitutes a good life. Uneasiness can rapidly give way to fear when residents are faced with losing the small-town ambience in such communities as Ellis, where people greet each other on the street. It's hardly surprising that breaking the rules, no matter how insignificantly, brings a swift and firm response. Maria was slightly anxious on her first night in Ellis alone and left the front stoop light on. Concerned, a neighbor called our landlord, Bess Swenson, the daughter of the home's owner. Bess had taken over caring for the house since her eighty-two-year-old mother had suffered a stroke the previous year and been confined to a nursing home. At around 9 p.m., Bess appeared at our door, noting that the neighbors had called, worried to see the light left on. Maria apologized, assuring her that despite this apparent carelessness, we were good tenants and neighbors.

Unfortunately, we failed to measure up to the Ellis standards of conduct again when we didn't mow the lawn after the grass had grown too long. To be honest, we thought the lawn looked fine and didn't want to waste gas. This time, our neighbor stopped in himself. First, he explained, our lawn was not as neat and tidy as the neighbors'. Next, he wanted to know if we knew how to use a lawnmower, and, if the answer was no—and something about our conduct made him suspect strongly it might be—he suggested that, for a small fee, one of his boys could cut the grass. Because Pat, a lifelong urbanite, had never even used a motorized lawnmower, Maria assured our neighbor that she would manage the job herself that weekend. If we changed our minds, he said, "My boys could do it, no problem." From then on, we took care of the grass every week. No one ever mentioned the matter again, but the first time Maria mowed the yard, she noticed our neighbor observing her from the side door next to his garage.

These sorts of interactions helped us experience some of the unique features of life in a small, isolated, and homogenous area. To be sure, Ellis is not the easiest place to be if you are a foreigner, gay, not Christian, not white, and obviously rich or poor. There is a certain tolerance for something new, but this often is a long way from being welcoming or embracing. There can be little question that openness increasingly will be an issue for many small towns, as immigration and the arrival of different people may offer the renewal and regeneration that will stave off extinction.

It is ironic that in Iowa, one of the whitest states in the nation,[45] where the distinctions between Lutheran and Catholic, German and Swedish, still hold large sway, strangers represent the best chance for the future and, simultaneously, the end of an old way of life. For people in Ellis, seeing the lone African American engineer who works at one of the town's plants, being treated by the South Asian doctor at the hospital, or doing business with the Jewish lawyer over in Dubuque are events that are often noted with the detached, scientific tone one might use to discuss the sighting of a rare flower or butterfly.

We were somewhat of a rarity ourselves, and Pat's being Irish, with spiky hair, round glasses, and a fondness for T-shirts that showcased bands such as The Pixies and The Smiths, did not make him stand out nearly as much as Maria. Back home, people who knew about Maria's background, her Greek father and West Indian mom, found the unusual pairing interesting in a cocktail-party conversation kind of way, while in Ellis, it caused a minor sensation. After one young woman finished her interview with us, she informed Maria that she "was as dark as she sounded on the phone." Another time, a local pastor came calling one night. After some talk about where we lived in Philadelphia and the state of our vegetable garden out back, the conversation turned, and he wondered, in a tone that sounded as if he was talking about the amount of rain this month, "Maria, now, I hear you're Hispanic." More than one person told us they had heard Maria was Polynesian. Maria started to preempt these questions by figuring out ways to work into the conversation that her last name was Greek. With the recent release of the film *My Big Fat Greek Wedding*, we had a useful, if over-the-top, popular-culture reference point.

Sometimes the interactions felt less benign and more unsettling. At mass one Sunday, when the priest called on the congregation to greet one another with "Peace be with you," we stood in silence as no one turned to shake our hands or acknowledge us in any way. Then there was the time Maria was walking home from town alone, wearing a white blouse, sandals, and a colorful cotton skirt. As she made her way off Main Street, a truck, replete with shotgun rack, slowed down. The two passengers, young men in their twenties who appeared to be heading home from work, gawked for ten very long seconds as she walked by. The truck's occupants never took their eyes off her; neither Maria, nor they, uttered a word. It was almost as though they were trying to figure out what new species had found its way to their town.

Such encounters offered a window into the struggles that lie ahead and reflected a controversy bubbling just below the surface throughout the rural Midwest. Back in 2000, then-governor Tom Vilsack initiated a public campaign to make his state "the new Ellis Island." It is no exaggeration to say that immigration in Iowa and much of the rural Midwest is not like anything witnessed before in New York, Chicago, or Boston.[46] "Outside of the cities, the Midwest is mostly 'the Old World transplanted to the New World,' a social system based on everyone acting and looking like everyone else."[47] Given the distinctive sensibilities of small Midwestern towns in Nebraska, Minnesota, Kansas, or Iowa, local life is built on the publicly uniform and fairly unanimous respect for law and on the comfort that comes from being surrounded by people who understand the rules of local life instinctively because they are the direct descendants of the people who created these standards. Small-town people rejoice in the fact that if you get in trouble, your neighbors will close ranks and reach out with aid. This was something we observed firsthand when a young mother in Ellis was paralyzed in a car accident the summer we lived there. As the medical bills started to pile up, the Rotary Club, churches, and neighbors coordinated collections and sponsored an all-you-can-eat waffle breakfast: the line out of the VFW Hall stretched down two blocks.

For now, the majority of Iowa's towns have no immigrants. People in places like Ellis have an accurate sense that when newcomers, namely immigrants, do arrive, their numbers will overtake these emptying-out towns with such breakneck speed that there hardly will be time for the people there to catch their breath.[48] In a single decade, Iowa towns such as Ottumwa, Postville, and Storm Lake transformed from homogenous populations to places where one in three residents was Hispanic, the vast majority of whom were not naturalized citizens.[49] And so, one of the reliable features of life here in Iowa, the thing that keeps so many close—that sense of comfort and familiarity—could disappear in a blink of an eye.

Outsiders who hear locals express worries about immigration might conclude that these anxieties reflect ignorance and prejudice. We believe that these anxieties reflect fears of changes looming on the horizon; small-town dwellers are frightened of losing what they know, and anxious that the things they hold dear will disappear and that no one but them will even care. Others have written about what happens when places such as Hazelton, Pennsylvania, and Denison and Postville, Iowa, face the onslaught of new arrivals—immigrants, "mostly Hispanic, largely dark-skinned, about half in the country illegally, without valid documents"—whose customs, language, and color mark them as alien and different.[50] Our book is different. We tell the story of a community with its arms outstretched, fumbling around in the dark, simply trying not to fall down.

Through the voices of young people, we chronicle the *real* story of small-town America. We take you into the lives of the young Iowans we met as they figured out whether to stay or go—what would be for many of them the most important decision of their lives. Yet it wasn't a decision made in an instant. Despite the romantic notions of the small-town kid eager to reinvent her- or himself, we find that leaving or staying is a gradual process that unfolds over a span of years, and we found scores of former and current Iowans who offered revealing insights into how they had come to take the paths they did. Those who left—Leavers—were distinctive in how much they valued their encounters with diversity and learning about a world "where not everyone is Lutheran." A self-styled "recovering Iowan" reflected on the pull for leaving small-town life in a *New York Times* letter to the editor: "I left Iowa after high school eight years ago in order to learn from a broader diversity of people and experiences than Iowa could offer. I cherished my Iowa roots but I needed to see the world."[51] But spend time with the people we dubbed Stayers and Returners, and it seems they take the opposite view. Of course, the outside world is exciting, but why would you want to trade in the known and understood for something that feels so uncertain? Underneath the Stayers' rah-rah boosterism for small-town life, one also detects a subtle feeling of rejection, an ambivalence toward places where life is strange and unpredictable.

The possible paths these young Iowans might take capture the dilemma of a twenty-first-century world in which people's life chances are defined so dramatically by their access to the education and skills necessary for the new economy. We talked with college graduates of the University of Iowa who have a six-in-ten chance of moving out of state once they complete a degree; the high school graduates who told us that they're lucky to earn $15 an hour building ambulances and assembling microprocessors; and the high school dropouts putting eggs in cartons, slaughtering hogs at the meat-processing plants, or walking the rows of corn during the harvest alongside undocumented workers. There were those who had served in the military, including several who were preparing to go overseas as part of Operation Enduring Freedom. And, of course, there were the lives that had taken unexpected turns: divorce, time in jail, drug abuse, and unplanned pregnancy and parenthood.

Against the backdrop of demographic shifts and rural outmigration there is a compelling story about the young people whose lives will determine the rural Heartland's fate. In the pages that follow, we will see how the crucial moment in these young Iowans' coming-of-age biographies would be when they decide to follow the paths that will make them Leavers, Stayers, or Returners. But the young people who follow one path or another are not randomly dotted across the landscape. Teachers, parents, and other influential adults cherry-pick the young people destined to leave and ignore the ones most likely to stay or return. Civic leaders may lament the rural youth exodus and the accompanying brain drain, but they fail to see how their own actions have helped create the problem. No one can deny that rural areas have less and less to offer their young people economically. Yet it hardly makes sense to expend time and energy on the cadre most likely to succeed *and* leave while neglecting the needs of the kids with fewer options and resources, the kids most likely to stay.

THE ACHIEVERS

One in five Ellis High graduates finds his or her way to West Point or the University of Iowa. This is no surprise, since Iowa students earn some of the nation's highest SAT and ACT scores. If you could travel back in time to their high school years, it seems that the young people who leave were the teachers' pets or, at the very least, the teachers' pet projects. The young people destined to be Achievers are the Ellis equivalent of a homegrown aristocracy. Kids whom the adults had written off because they would never amount to enough to get out of Liberty County[52] got letters home and detention for missed classes or assignments, while the Achievers consistently escaped such punishments. Most, but not all, of the kids who attended universities were like Sonya Eden,[53] a journalism major now working at a museum in Philadelphia whose mother and father attended college themselves. But other kids came from families in which college would not be a likely destination without direct encouragement from assorted interested adults outside the family. Being one of the students whom the teachers and staff treated differently had the power to change a young person's future: their talents and ability made them recipients of their teachers' and neighbors' attention. Those kids were placed on a different trajectory because the entire town was behind them, cheering for them to make it and supporting them in concrete ways. These young people had the sense that the town's inhabitants instilled all their hopes, best wishes, and expectations in their futures. One of the abiding truths of small-town life is that people want to say they knew the local kid before he or she made it big.

The good news for those among the chosen few is that the school could operate as a meritocracy where talent and drive were identified and rewarded. Yet since fewer than half of the Achievers will live in Iowa after earning their degree, the whole system suffers from an undeniable inefficiency. Paying so much attention to the Achievers drains Ellis's resources, as it serves young people who are least likely to give anything back to the town.

THE STAYERS

In an era in which so many twenty-somethings suffer from "failure to launch" syndrome, Stayers' most unique characteristic may be how quickly they start looking and acting like adults. They transition to adulthood and families, jobs, and grown-up lives far more quickly than their peers who out-migrate. A relatively cheap cost of living makes it easier for young people to afford the accoutrements of adulthood. The other key to avoiding the pitfalls of extended adolescence is that Stayers do not attend college. Twenty-somethings coming of age in small towns can still find jobs in blue-collar occupations such as factory work, auto repair, and construction. The conundrum is that many of these jobs are particularly prone to stagnating wages, disappearing benefits, and downsizing.[54] And within a decade of leaving high school, nearly one-fifth of the young people we studied who were Stayers had stopped their education and had never lived anywhere but Ellis or Liberty County. Forgoing college for a job at the plant or as a truck driver is, over the long haul, a precarious place to be economically.

A machine operator living in Ellis complains about the struggles facing old-fashioned workers who find themselves trapped in a newfangled economy. The tragedy is that, in time, Stayers come to realize that not having a college degree hurts them as they face a future of downward mobility and grave uncertainty. Stayers are the most visible vestige of the hollowing-out problem. They are also a group that is ignored in the policy discussions about how to save the rural Heartland. There is no question that Ellis's Stayers are grappling with a languishing economy, a dying small town, and a fading way of life. However, the only policies pursued at the local and state levels are aimed at attracting back the educated leavers, which ignores both the untapped resource of the people who stayed and the part that adults played in pushing a select group of kids to leave in the first place.

THE SEEKERS

"Some people ain't made for small-town living," observes Doc Gibbons in Thornton Wilder's classic *Our Town*, and, indeed, the Seekers devote their childhood and teenage years to plotting their escapes. Whereas the Achievers leave because everyone expects them to, for the Seekers, fleeing their small town is something they feel compelled to do. Garrison Keillor, that famous observer of small-town life, writes, "Leaving home is a kind of forgiveness. . . . You can start over." It is, in the truest sense, "a sort of redemption."[55] For the Seekers the most common pathway out of Iowa is via military service. Of a graduating class of forty students, Ellis High School records show that at least 10 percent of every class enlists annually. That percentage of young people joining the armed forces has stayed the same, and even increased, since the wars in Iraq and Afghanistan began.

Those headed to the military were never destined for college—not because they don't want a degree, but because their parents can't afford it. Neither the best nor the worst students, they are also not the most affluent or the poorest. Talk with their teachers, advisers, and coaches and you learn they are the solid kids: not the captain of the football team, but maybe the second-string player who served the team faithfully every season. They may lack the grades and money to attend the University of Iowa, but they have no desire to settle into married life with their high school sweetheart or get a dead-end job. And, in old age, when they reflect on their lives, they don't want to regret missed opportunities: not seeing the rest of the country or the world, never taking a plane to an exotic destination, never seeing the ocean.

THE RETURNERS: HIGH-FLYERS AND BOOMERANGS

When people manage to pay attention to the rural youth exodus, they focus on a select group of Returners we call the High-Flyers —those twenty-somethings who return to small towns armed with college degrees and entrepreneurial ambitions. These are the men and women whom Iowa's boosters long to bring back home. But when you hear the stories of how these journeys ended—that is, where they started, back home in Ellis—it is hard to imagine how the state can lure many Iowans back to the countryside with the promise of venture capital and bike paths. A very select sort of kid, on track to be the quintessential, college-bound, ambitious Achiever, uses the college years to figure out that big-city life is not what he or she wants or needs and, ultimately, opts to reverse course. Surrounded by valedictorians, captains of the lacrosse team, and suburbanites who took calculus in high school and spent their summers in Europe, Returners abandon the Achiever trajectory. They describe college as a time when they could not find their footing and became increasingly disillusioned with a world that had seemed so appealing when it was just a daydream.

Even though they maintained their grades and earned a degree, college seemed to test their suitability for the outside world, and being away from home took an emotional and psychic toll. Although the high-achieving Leavers and Seekers value their encounters with diversity and come to see small towns as limited and closed, Returners say that the same sorts of experiences—being surrounded by strangers and living a fast-paced life—frustrated them. They found what lay beyond Ellis unwelcoming and disorienting and, given the choice, prioritize the familiar over the possibility of something else.

Although the High-Flyers are the ones to whom politicians market the state, our time in Ellis revealed that most of the Iowans coming home are the Boomerangs: young people who have far more in common with the Stayers than the Achievers. The Boomerangs' numbers include former enlisted men and women who move back to Iowa after leaving the armed forces and the mostly female graduates of community colleges. For the typical Boomerangs attending community college, leaving Ellis was only to be a temporary situation from the outset. While their friends at the University of Iowa were choosing a major, celebrating the fact that they no longer needed fake IDs, and pledging fraternities and sororities, Boomerangs, who tend to be young women, graduated from their two-year programs in accounting or nursing and acquired husbands, full-time jobs, and mortgages—in short, they eagerly embarked upon genuinely grown-up lives. Boomerangs are in a rush to start a "real life"; they will tell you they have little interest in backpacking through Europe or renting a tiny apartment with a roommate and waitressing until they find their dream career. They have chosen the safe and familiar, and, like young people of another time, they have no desire to delay pursuing the more traditional goals of early adulthood: marriage and family.

Ultimately, the most important lessons the Stayers, Leavers, and Returners can teach us is that small towns play an unwitting part in their own decline. Teachers, parents, and neighbors feel obligated to push and prod the talented kids to succeed, yet, when their best and brightest follow their advice, the investment the community has made in them becomes a boon for someplace else, while the remaining young people are neither afforded the same attention nor groomed for success of any kind. Whether this is willful neglect or a rational deployment of resources, the result is the same: small towns such as Ellis have become trapped by their self-fulfilling prophecies. Perhaps the optimistic Heartland mythology—farmers always believe that the next season will be better—is one reason that people in towns like Ellis don't advertise how difficult things have become.

The national debates about failing communities and economic downturns make it sound as if only cities are vulnerable. Politicians shout *over* the rural crisis in the culture wars: either there's the rhetoric about the "real" and patriotic small-town America[56] or a blaming-the-victim discussion ensues about bitter, close-minded, and racist rural America.[57]

In the words of former U.S. Rep. Robin Hayes of North Carolina, "The real Americans . . . work and accomplish and achieve and believe in God." And, indeed, the grand illusion of the mythic rural America gets perpetuated easily. On drives through the countryside and small towns, visitors fail to see that the abandoned barns and quiet Main Streets are symptoms of a decaying way of life in just the same way that burned-out buildings and forgotten urban neighborhoods are monuments to the city's moral and economic decline. The typical imagery of the countryside that adorns coins and stamps embodies all that is right with America—versus the inner city, which symbolizes all that is wrong. They would have us believe, writes the *Wall Street Journal's* Thomas Frank, that "the country is divided into a land of the soulful, hard-working producers and a land of the paper-pushing parasites; a plain-spoken heartland and the sinister big cities." [59] In the big city, it is true, young men sling dime bags on corners in front of vacant buildings, whereas in the rural Heartland, dealers cook meth using salvaged cars and illegally purchased cough syrup at abandoned barns. In the public's imagination, teen mothers exist only in the ghetto, and yet young mothers of the countryside share many of the characteristics of their vilified urban counterparts. Both types of family end up on welfare. Rural young mothers differ only in the order in which they do things; they will wed their children's fathers and then become single mothers *after* a divorce.[60] In each place, there is no shortage of guns: it is just that in the inner city, those guns are illegal, while in small towns shotguns get displayed in the backs of trucks or in polished oak cabinets not far from the family china.

In the end, young people from the countryside (just like the ones in the city) who have talent and earn scholarships get air-lifted out to fulfill their potential someplace else. Back home, those with the fewest options and resources face trying to compete in an economy in which the rules keep getting changed in the middle of the game. The young people who are in-between, the Returners, might come home after the outside world fails to live up to its promise and bet their futures on their hometown holding on just a little bit longer. Others, desperate to free themselves from what they see as the limitations of a small-town existence, volunteer to fight for America, just because heading to war offers something more than getting trapped in the countryside.

In sum, the *real* America of the Heartland hangs in the balance because of massive global market transformations, and the agriculture and manufacturing sectors' compulsive efforts to eliminate human workers, deskill their jobs, and replace them with technology; and because crime is on the rise, along with drug use; poverty is spreading—and communities and families are coming apart at the seams. Maybe the most useful insight comes from Richard Russo, the Pulitzer Prize–winning author who believes that any story of small-town America is, at its core, the story of the people who stay and the ones who go. Even for young people who leave, there is always a "ghost version" of yourself who can be found "sitting at the bar . . . watching those long-neck bottles of beer line up sweating in front of you." And, for those who stay, small-town life has become a place "where people are hanging on to home and hanging onto pride, and hanging on by a thread."[61]

ONE

The Achievers

*I did a very un-Kansas thing: I started voting Democratic.
And then I did something that, I have since found, was
utterly typical of my generation of college-educated
Kansans: I left.*

—Thomas Frank, What's the Matter with Kansas?
How Conservatives Won the Heart of America

RICHARD GRUNSKY IS AN ORDERED MAN. This is reflected in his sturdy wardrobe—which looks as though it might have been purchased in the Sears Men's Department in Cedar Rapids—and in the tidy appearance of his corner office, which also doubles as Ellis High School's guidance center. Seated at his swivel desk chair, by a window overlooking the school's gravel parking lot, Grunsky has heard it all. Here students recount for him their triumphs—college scholarships, news of a job, high ACT scores—and also their traumas: drug problems, legal troubles, thoughts of suicide, unplanned and unwanted pregnancies, physical or sexual abuse, a family's financial or emotional collapse. Since Ellis is an hour's drive from the nearest approximation of a city, and the Ellis high school lacks a clinical psychologist or social worker on the full-time staff, Grunsky, the school's only guidance counselor, is very much alone on the front lines.

With graduation just a few months away, Grunsky is ticking off the days until he turns in the keys to his office of more than twenty years. When you've worked long enough to see the kids who once sat in your office grow into the parents of the students currently walking the hallways, it's time to go. On the brink of his retirement, Grunsky has the air of a man who's satisfied that he has done his job well but who is content to be moving on.

Though Grunsky is part of a generation of teachers who weren't obsessed with evaluation and assessment, he has changed with the times. The current principal of the school, George Herdemann, is a stickler for numbers, trends, and percentage points of increases and declines, and he counts himself among No Child Left Behind–era administrators. Once Herdemann became principal, Grunsky's job responsibilities expanded to include that of school statistician. As such, the annual survey of the senior class is not the most scientific of undertakings. During the final week of school, Grunsky gathers the seniors together one last time, and he goes around the room asking each of them about their postgraduation plans. Because this is a small country school and because Grunsky has been their sole counselor, there are few surprises. The best students—who are, more often than not, the sons and daughters of the town's professional class—are headed for the state's crown-jewel public universities: Iowa State and the University of Iowa. A smaller number will go to the small, private Lutheran schools that some of their parents attended. The less overachieving college-bound kids might find their way to the second- and third-tier "suitcase" schools of Northern Iowa and Upper Iowa University, but those kids caught right in the fat part of the bell curve mostly enroll in community colleges. One in ten male seniors enlists in the armed services, and the rest of the non-college-bound will go straight into the region's blue-collar workforce.

A few respond with uncertainty about their plans; some will likely start working, and others may find themselves skirting the law in the region's underground world of meth dealing and using. Year after year, Grunsky collects the data on postgraduation plans in the form of legal-pad pages filled with handwritten notes kept in a manila folder, which is eventually filed away in a tall metal cabinet. Grunsky doesn't need pie charts and bar graphs to reveal the patterns; his surveys can be read like a blueprint for the social machinery of levers, gears, and pedals driving a select minority of kids away and keeping the rest close to home.[1] Who leaves Ellis? "The best kids go," he explains, "while the ones with the biggest problems stay, and then, we have to deal with *their* kids in the schools in the next generation."

The "best kids" are the high-achieving, most-likely-to-succeed students destined for highly regarded colleges, a group we have termed the Achievers. Their families, teachers, neighbors, and coaches have raised them with a sense of manifest destiny about how their lives will unfold. What makes the college-bound Achievers distinct from other Iowans who leave is that they generally do not come home except for Thanksgiving or to celebrate the occasional wedding. The longer they're gone, the harder it is to readjust because they become accustomed to another life, often one with tempting options such as diverse cuisine and more varied shopping. They start locking their front doors and forgetting to greet people on the street with a warm hello, and their ability to follow the rules of a small town evaporates, becoming just another habit from childhood they put aside. After significant time away, they can't recall how they ever lived out in the middle of nowhere. Worst of all, they may start to see Ellis the way outsiders do: parochial and just a little redneck.

• • •

The young people destined to leave Ellis—the ones who are widely blamed for the rural brain drain—are quite special, and it seems that Dick Grunsky has a valid point. The Achievers' ranks include the class valedictorians and the first chairs from the orchestra, the track stars and student-government leaders. Their talents and accomplishments earned them regular coverage in the local newspaper, and folks in town glow with pride when the Achievers' names get mentioned over early-bird specials at the Ellis Cafe. The people of Ellis glean tremendous satisfaction from the fact that they are good at raising kids. Unfortunately, the homegrown best and brightest move away to be successes someplace else: of the forty or fifty freshmen, fewer than twenty will still live in and around Liberty County within a decade after graduating from high school.

Under the rules of the school's hierarchy, the Achievers were the winners of a rigged competition. Not only did they bask in adult praise, they received special treatment, and different rules applied to them. Although some other kids got the message from teachers that they were good-for-nothings who lacked that spark to make it in New York or Chicago, the Achievers—singled out for futures that would lead them far from the countryside—could do no wrong. These high-achieving ex-Iowans spent their adolescence being cultivated[2] by well-intentioned adults who never gave them a chance to settle for the easy or predictable route. At times, this grooming takes form as a subtle steering toward activities and pursuits that would enrich and prepare the Achievers for life beyond Ellis. At other times, the directives were more overt. For example, parents often prohibited these young people from working too much at a job so that they could focus on the extracurricular activities that would help get them into college. The teachers, coaches, and parents of Achievers advised them to do something to fatten their résumés instead of spending summer vacations hanging out with their friends. As part of the process that leads young people down one path or another, the young people who are "chosen" get the message that it is their fate, indeed their duty, to leave small-town life behind. It was as if the whole town "had your back" and "wanted you to go on," recalls a star basketball player for the Ellis Hawks championship squad who became the first person in her family to set foot on a college campus.

The most striking feature of the Achievers' lives is how all of them get so much of their teachers'—and everyone else's—positive attention. The young people who grow up to be Achievers spend their teenage years having their successes, quite literally, put up in lights. In Ellis, this means an old-fashioned movie-marquee-style sign outside Dunbar's hardware store on Main Street. The Achievers discover that earning good grades, displaying good behavior, and being praised in front of their classmates can grant special privileges and access to adults who can help them break free of small-town life. In short, they absorb everyone's expectations into their sense of self. With these hopes comes the belief that the local kids' accomplishments reflect back on all the people who touched their life before they made it.[3]

Ellis's pastoral setting belies a world where class matters just as much, if not more, than it does in other milieus. From inner-city ghettoes to upscale gated communities, the majority of Americans inhabit social worlds marked by little economic heterogeneity. But here in rural America, the lower, working, middle, and upper classes cannot escape one another when they shop for groceries, attend church, or cheer on the local stars at homecoming. Paradoxically, although sharing such cramped quarters creates more opportunities for social contact, it also increases the need for individuals to mark out the clearest sorts of social boundaries between people from the right and wrong sides of Railroad or Division street. And there is probably no other place in American society where the rules of class and status play out with a more brutal efficiency than in the world of a country high school. The sociologist Murray Milner, noted for his studies of Indian society, draws an intriguing parallel between adolescent culture's pecking order and the Indian caste system. Despite all the pain the school causes its "untouchables," Milner observes, for its Brahmin caste—that is, those at the top—the school is a scene of triumphs.[4] In Ellis, this is *uniquely* true. We doubt it will surprise anyone that most of the best kids Dick Grunsky says will leave Ellis also live in the section of town known, to those who do not live there, as "Snob Hill" and come from the town's most privileged families. Take Megan Frank, the daughter of a local businessman earning her MBA so she can pursue a career in hospital administration in her adopted hometown of Indianapolis. Back in high school, Megan was one of the pretty and popular girls who, on occasion, wielded "mean girl" influence. As a member of the Homecoming Court and the editor of the yearbook, Megan sat at the top of Ellis's unofficial social register. As she recalls, the hierarchy revolved around last names: "You've always known from growing up whose parents had money, and I guess, in a way, depending on what your last name was, depended on whether you were popular or not, or if your teachers would like you in school. It seemed like that to me. If you got into swing choir or if you got into the National Honor Society, I mean, you kind of knew. You just knew. That's just the way it was."

The myth of egalitarianism that permeates American consciousness insists that educational institutions offer objective measures of a student's potential, and once talent gets measured and recognized, those employed by the schools reward diligence and achievement by providing opportunities for pull-yourself-up-by-the-bootstrap-style success. In reality, the system tends to place children of the elite in a position of privilege from the start, and the offspring of parents with more modest circumstances aren't afforded the same initial advantages.[5] When the French sociologist Pierre Bourdieu describes the power of social class and status in everyday life, he tells us that individuals acquire and deploy their cultural assets to manage their position in the social order. One of the most important marketplaces for spending and earning this special sort of wealth is in the setting of a school.[6] It is here that individuals rely on their access to this most precious insider knowledge to determine who gets ahead or is left behind. Dick Grunsky and the rest of the teachers at the high school oversee the critical stage in the sifting and sorting system that leads *some* young people away and ensures that others stay closer to home. Whether they're fair or not, these preliminary judgments seem to hang over young people's heads, and in the words of one college graduate now living in the Twin Cities, they fuel the sense that, in Ellis, one's fate was set "before you walked into kindergarten on the first day of school."[7]

Although the kids from prominent families, like Megan Frank, readily admit they had an early lead in the race to succeed, some Achievers come from far more humble origins, and, occasionally, the storied meritocracy actually becomes a reality. Kids without privilege and connections but with talent and potential—and the "right" kind of underprivileged family—get the chance to follow a different path. For these young people, being talented was not sufficient reason to set them on the leaving path. Teachers, parents, and other influential adults vetted them to assess their worthiness. A talented kid not from the best part of town could be groomed as an Achiever as long as neighbors assessed the young person's circumstances to be a result of misfortune rather than moral failure or fecklessness, and as long as his or her family was not judged to be undeserving of local philanthropy. Their immediate relatives couldn't include *too many* ne'er-do-wells, wife beaters, or drunks. If such individuals were close family members, such conduct had to be viewed as an aberration, rather than an observable pattern within multiple generations. Ideally, the student's family was counted among the respectable, churchgoing sort, even if the church they attended was among the lower Protestant churches rather than the mainstream Lutheran and Catholic ones. Respectability could be earned through any number of simple acts: not wasting food stamps or unemployment checks at the supermarket, or wearing clean and mended clothes, even if they were old and purchased at the discount store.

Under this precise set of conditions, these students become the real-life Charlotte Simmonses—the eponymous heroine of Tom Wolfe's novel who escapes the limited prospects of life in a fading Blue Ridge Mountains town after she wins a scholarship to a fictional version of Duke.[8] Like Wolfe's character, Ellis's Achievers of more modest means are set on a special track by teachers who believe their gifts have marked them as destined for something beyond Liberty County. Judgments about young people's potential are made even before they enter elementary school, when they first start to offer clues about their personality and promise. Parents, relatives, friends, and neighbors act like oracles, looking into crystal balls and reading palms, trying to tell the fortune of Ellis's young people: which among them will "stay on the farm" and "marry their high school sweetheart" and which ones "have the drive" and inclination to leave. Of course, it is impossible to know which of these assessments are prescient, which are self-fulfilling prophecies, or which are just plain wide of the mark. At times, the process of privileging the talented has the potential to divide families, because while one child is singled out, others might be viewed as unworthy of extra attention.

Unlike his classmates who roll out of bed and don sweats and jeans for their classes, third-year University of Iowa Law School student Jack Pederson prefers a more buttoned-down look. With Dockers slacks and collared shirts, Jack dresses as if he's heading off to the office, not a lecture. Jack believes that first impressions matter; besides, he isn't like the majority of his classmates, whose affluence and privilege never gave them any reason to doubt that they would earn a prestigious high-powered degree. For Jack, upward mobility has come through long-term strategic planning, not as a birthright.

Of the three kids in his family, Jack will be the only one to experience life on the quads of a Big 10 university. From the very start, Jack's parents—June, a dental hygienist, and Warren, a hog farmer—wanted the best for all of their children. But the Pedersons, who had no experience with higher education (beyond June's community college courses to be a dental hygienist), took a decidedly hands-off approach. Jack says that back in high school, "[Mom and Dad] never said a thing about going to college and having a career. This doesn't mean they didn't care, but they knew I would do whatever I wanted to do." According to Jack, no coach or teacher pushed him to get out of Ellis. Yet, by the time he was in high school, his high scores on standardized tests alerted teachers to his above-average intelligence, whereas his sister and brother never demonstrated the same ability. "Basically, it's kind of one of those stories where I nailed every test, and, growing up, my brother and sister struggled," he says. So through a mixture of divination and careful deployment of resources, these assessments inched the three kids in different directions. Starting in high school, Jack's brother and sister took part-time jobs throughout the school year; Jack only worked on his father's farm in the summer months. From September through June, "it was understood" that homework, baseball, Student Senate, and the National Honor Society would be Jack's main pursuits. "It was kind of always predetermined that—no, it wasn't predetermined, it was just wherever we wanted to go, and [my family] kind of understood that my interests would take me away, while I think they understood my brother and sister would stay there."

Looking back, Jack says the main driver that got him to college and law school was this unwavering conviction that he would be one of those kids to leave. And though he underplays the role of his high school teachers, they were the ones who decided Jack was talented in the first place and told his parents to expect great things from *this* kid.

Jonathan Garman meets us at a coffee shop not far from his apartment in the trendy section of Washington, D.C., known as Adams Morgan, a neighborhood that stands out because of its bohemian edge in a city that leans to the formal and stuffy. Jonathan takes a seat. As the young aide to a Republican senator, we recognize him immediately; he is clean-cut and well-scrubbed, wearing a tie, all business.

In their autobiographies, Achievers such as Jonathan and Jack tell an eminently pleasing and self-satisfying story of how, through their own Horatio Alger efforts, they excelled. Like Jack, neither of Jonathan's parents had attended college: getting a degree was something, Jonathan recalls, that his mother and father "just left in our hands." There was never any sort of disappointment or recrimination directed at either of their sons' varying outcomes. Jonathan's oldest brother "went from high school to community college" and "wanted to get married," while Jonathan headed off to Grinnell College. The sifting and sorting system pushing him away and keeping his sibling close seemed to unfold through a collection of choices he and his brother *appeared* to make for themselves. Yet, just like Jack, Jonathan describes how efforts behind the scenes pushed him toward college and supplemented his parents' well-meaning, if hands-off, higher-education aspirations. So even though Jonathan insists that his grades and scores earned him this place in college, and they surely did, he also acknowledges that several people outside his immediate family kept him on track during his crucial high school years. First, there was Mrs. Pulsin, the high school's English teacher, who taught reading, English, and a couple other courses. Jonathan recounts, "She is actually the one who introduced me to the scholarship opportunity to go to Germany," which would change his life and inspire him to study politics and international relations in college. After the school eliminated the German-language program in a round of budget cuts, Mrs. Pulsin used her free period to tutor Jonathan privately in German for an entire school year.

Then there was the school nurse, Sandi Weiland, the mom of one of Jonathan's classmates. For a special group of kids, Jonathan included, Mrs. Weiland served as the "unofficial" guidance counselor. As long as no one was sick or needed her attention, the kids went to her office and plopped themselves in the comfortable waiting-room chairs as she worked quietly at her desk. Jonathan says he and his friends gathered there to gossip, discuss their favorite TV shows, or study. Mrs. Weiland's office epitomized one of the best parts of attending a small country school; as Jonathan explains, "The teachers just knew everybody and where people were coming from." For the kids fortunate enough to receive it, this one-on-one time outside of class could be the greatest gift. The trouble is that for the young people who were not bound for college or who didn't earn the high test scores, memories like these don't exist.

Though the school plays a central role in cultivating the talents of Achievers, the wider community is also intricately involved in preparing them. There is an abiding sense in places like Ellis that you want to see "somebody from a small town make it big," and if you can play some part in that sort of success, "then that would be just wonderful." Along with the special treatment that Achievers received came the added weight of their hometown's hopes. Even as the people around them assured the Achievers that they had earned that special treatment, it was hard not to feel guilty about being set apart or to feel burdened by all the great expectations.

Yet, with time, the Achievers say they subsumed these dreams into their identities. The support of the people back home made them believe they could accomplish anything.

Ella Frankel, a graduate student earning her doctorate in theology in St. Louis, grew up on a dairy farm just outside of town. The second of six children, she is twenty-five years old, but her youngest sister is eight and just started second grade. Ella's mom, whom we met during our time in Ellis, gave her daughter the pale blue eyes, now hidden behind glasses. She studied to be a teacher before she became a farmer's wife.

Just like so many other Achievers, the process of being singled out left an indelible impression on Ella, and long before she became her class's valedictorian, she remembers her teachers and parents noticing her academic gifts. Growing up in Ellis, she felt "embraced by the community and kind of set forth to go do something with what I had been given." Although some of her classmates settled down quickly into lives that looked no different from the lives of their parents or grandparents, she felt it was her responsibility "to experience a lot more than high school." More than anything else, Ella's family and teachers would tell her they wanted her "to continue to develop and grow" into the person that they believed Ella's gifts "called [her] to be," because Ellis "was only the beginning." Ella also understood "that that's not necessarily how it is or how it is supposed to be for other people. That there are people who can be happy" remaining close to home. But Ella absorbed the sense that she was not raised to be one of them.

Rose Rolland was one of the poor farm kids who came to school clean but wearing the sorts of clothes "everyone knew" her mom had gotten from the thrift store. During the depths of the farm crisis, when the Rollands had no money for anything but bread, sugar, and coffee, all the food the family consumed came from the farm. When things got tougher, and there was no money for clothes, even used ones, Rose's winter boots consisted of plastic bread sacks wrapped around last year's shoes. Sporting Wonderbread logos instead of the trendy Nike swoosh forced Rose to acquire a certain toughness. The ebbs and flows of her family's economic fortunes were well known to folks in town, and the Rollands' situation was widely considered a result of bad luck and unfortunate timing, rather than a failing of character. It helped that Rose, like her mother and oldest brother, had always done well in school; by the time Rose enrolled in high school, she was among her class's most popular girls and an honors student demonstrating a particular aptitude for math and science.

Rose would soon become one teacher's pet—the first step in the process of being set apart as an Achiever. As one of the popular kids at school, Rose discovered that different rules applied to her and to the town's privileged sons and daughters. "I mean, I could always do anything. I didn't, but I got away with stuff that I know I shouldn't have, that the other kids couldn't have." When Rose earned top scores on her ACTs, a letter from Cornell University promptly arrived in the mail. Cornell's engineering program was eager to recruit women and minorities, and Rose's scores were high enough to earn her a special invitation to apply. She did, and in April she found herself deciding between the Ivy League and the University of Iowa. For most kids from an average city suburb, there would have been little need for deliberation.

But for kids coming of age in Ellis, where *U.S. News and World Report* rankings of the nation's colleges exist outside the consciousness of most folks, there were other considerations. Historically, Ellis's brightest students have attended the University of Iowa or Iowa State. Not only were the Achievers and their teachers somewhat naïve about the college admissions game, but the major concern for Rose, like many other kids from Iowa, was money. On paper, farmers and landowners—even the ones who have no discernible income and who are drowning in debt—appear to be quite solvent because of their property and assets. Since many farmers are land-rich but cash-poor, their children can expect to receive precious little aid for college. Compounding the problem is the fact that most farmers carry such a high burden of debt. By the early 1990s, no bank manager, or farmer for that matter, was eager to take on more loans even to send their children to college—even an ivy-covered one. Public universities are not simply the best option; given the calculus of financial-aid eligibility, they become the only one.

Like the other Achievers coming from farm families, Rose understood that going to school would require her to work full time. While at the University of Iowa, she held jobs in fast-food restaurants in Iowa City: McDonald's, Pizza Hut, and Dairy Queen, where she became the night manager. She wondered if there would ever be a time in her life when her clothes and hair would not smell of grease. Her college education, made possible by the state of Iowa and "the good people at Dairy Queen," ended when she graduated with a teacher's degree and married one of her classmates, a former basketball player who had grown up in Maryland and who was on track for a career as a stockbroker.

Rose's desire to become a teacher stems from her deep and profound belief in the power of education to transform young people's lives, and it is, in part, a tribute to her teachers. When we interviewed her, a decade after leaving Ellis, it was the first time since she was eighteen that Rose was *not* bringing home a paycheck. She'd just had her first baby and was able to take a few months off from teaching to stay home. All the struggles and hardships of her childhood and adolescence seemed a far cry from her new life of upscale comfort and privilege in the D.C. suburbs. Recently, she and her financial-consultant husband had purchased a starter home for half a million dollars; they could have bought an identical house back in Ellis for less than $100,000. Rose still has not digested the realities of this new life more than a thousand miles from her parents' farm. Wearing designer labels and buying high-end baby toys still feels decadent to her, even now that she can afford Nikes for her son. Playing with the baby on the polished hardwood floors of her ranch-style house, which is decorated throughout with brand-new Shaker-style furniture, Rose muses that "my husband laughs at me all the time" because part of her still cannot quite reconcile the affluence of this new life with her Iowa farmgirl past.

One might assume that kids coming of age in places like Ellis might be counting off the days until they can leave, but the reality is that leaving is a gradual process that most young people must be persuaded to undertake: years of planning and preparation go into making a new life someplace else. And for the Achievers, leaving behind the familiar world in which they've been so successful is a difficult transition, evoking feelings of heartache and loss alongside excitement and anticipation. What the Achievers will remember most are the parents, aunts, uncles, neighbors, and teachers who believed in them. When people are loved, supported, and at ease, moving away is not their natural priority, but these concerned adults convinced the Achievers that they owed it to themselves and to the people they left behind to experience the world.

Before Marcy Trillin was a graduate student at Stanford completing her doctorate in statistics, she was the only daughter of Ellis's Lutheran pastor. Cautious with her words and highly intelligent, Marcy grew up understanding that a minister's kid would be held to a higher standard and that she had two options: work harder and live up to public expectations, or rebel completely and be the biggest troublemaker in town. Marcy chose the former.

Marcy's parents settled in Ellis when she was a baby. They have been residents there for more than twenty years, but some locals still might consider them interlopers. Perhaps because her parents' roots were not so deep in town or because they had college degrees themselves, Marcy says, her parents never believed she would stay in the countryside. "Definitely, my mother always wanted me to move away. She'd always say, 'Don't stay in Ellis.' She would tell me that ... she always felt confined and a little bored by her life. I think she knew I was missing opportunities and there was more to offer in other places."

And so, parents like Marcy's mother find themselves caught in a troubling conundrum because they, more than anyone else, invest so much in the young people destined to be Achievers. Parents love and care for their children and raise them to be strong enough to leave and forge a life independent from their family. As any parent understands, this is parenting's fundamental dilemma. But in places such as Ellis, helping children succeed does not simply mean they leave their families; they also leave behind a community that has provided them with so much and that, quite possibly, will not be able to survive without them.

Another key strategy these families use to get their young people ahead is to delay their entry into the labor force. For high-achieving college-bound kids, the high school years are a time to beef up GPAs and accumulate extracurricular accomplishments. Being at school before and after classes enables the future Achievers to strengthen all-important connections to teachers and coaches, whose support will be crucial as the students apply and transition to college. But for working- and lower-class young people, whose need to work can be greater, a parent or teacher must convince them of the long-term benefits of investing in school rather than devoting their energy to earning money for the props of adolescent life: cars, clothes, sneakers, and entertainment.

Regardless of their backgrounds, young people who spend time in extracurricular activities often need their parents to cover the expenses of the teenage years. "My parents never expected us to

work," explains Angela Zimmer, a recent University of Iowa graduate. "It was just assumed" that none of the family's three daughters
would be distracted by after-school jobs. Their mom, Cindi, worked
full time when the girls entered grammar school. The job kept her
away from home, but it also meant that her daughters never lacked
money for the things that help teenagers fit in with their friends,
especially the ones with money who are headed off to college. After
Angela's oldest sister, Becca, won a scholarship to the University
of Iowa, it was as if Angela's parents, who did not attend college
themselves, had cracked a secret code for getting their kids to end
up like the sons and daughters of the local Ellis aristocrats. It helped
that all the Zimmer girls were pretty, above-average athletes, and
strong students, and that their parents are respected members of
their church and active in the school community. Everything about
the way the family operated "steered us more toward college." This
was different from many of Angela's friends, who, Angela said,
people "just knew" would be getting married and staying in Ellis
after high school; they would "just get a job and never leave."

GOING OFF TO COLLEGE

After finishing high school, attending college is the next and most
noteworthy step in the gradual process of leaving. The costs of
higher education elsewhere and the existence of Iowa's fine university and college system mean that many Achievers do not leave
Iowa until after they collect a college diploma. There is no question
that moving into a college dorm is a quintessential young-adult rite
of passage for an ever-increasing number of eighteen-year-olds.[9]
All college freshmen are caught between the wider adult world
and their teenage social world, where their identities were defined
by their families, high school, and town. But for small-town kids,
particularly from the countryside, going off to college is a momentous, intense, and, for some, alienating experience.

Growing up in a sheltered small town means that the temptations of a wild college party scene can prove distracting, and some
people we spoke to admitted that their college social lives over-
took their academic pursuits. Moreover, they often faced a serious adjustment as they settled in with new peer groups. For many
small-town kids, dorm life brings them into contact with a level of
privilege unlike any they have seen before. Some young people feel
uncomfortable trading in flannel shirts and blue jeans for designer
labels and Coach bags, although others embrace the change. For
Achievers such as Rose, these hallmarks of privilege stand in even
starker contrast to their own upbringing. Others are unwilling to
break ties to friends and family, especially boyfriends or girlfriends
back home. A few people we interviewed said that they simply were
not willing to reinvent themselves or give up the familiarity and
comforts of small-town life—such as never being surrounded by
strangers or being the big fish in a little pond. College is the Achiever's point of entry into a world controlled by the nation's elite; like
so many other tests in life, some people are more prepared to tackle
them than others.[10] The Leavers who adjust more easily to college
life use higher education as a stepping-stone to or dress rehearsal
for their new lives; after more time away from home, they see their
hometowns through outsiders' eyes, and with time the rules of life
in the countryside start to chafe.

Even those Achievers who fit in more seamlessly than do their
peers experience growing pains. Often, the newfound freedom of a
world without the type of close supervision they were accustomed
to means they must police their own behavior and trust their own
judgment. They learn quickly that they must balance the studied re-
straint of their upbringing with the freedoms afforded by a campus
lifestyle. In their first brushes with the world beyond Ellis, many
young people find it difficult to be surrounded by concrete buildings, far from the land. Of course, there are also the first awkward

encounters with the givens of college life: conspicuous consumption, Animal House–style debauchery, and a social world ruled by rich kids whose parents foot their credit-card bills. Under any conditions, when young people from such varied backgrounds live together in a dorm, there will be misunderstandings and differing expectations. Ignorance about the rules of college life transforms Ellis's former popular students and teachers' pets—overnight—into country bumpkins.[11]

For Angela Zimmer, the first encounters with "rich kids" at college were a test of self-confidence. Arriving on campus was a culture shock, not simply because of the apparent ubiquity of illicit drugs and Victoria's Secret–themed parties where female guests wear lingerie, but because of how her peers treated her. At the University of Iowa, Angela says, you could easily pick out the country kids. They were drawn to one another because "we just stood out" in terms of how they carried themselves and looked. In the dorms, when Angela shared stories about going hunting with her father or listened to country music while doing her homework, the girls on her floor "would kind of look at you like, you know, it's weird." In their eyes, Angela, the softball star and honor student from the town no one had heard of, was little more than a "hick" and, confesses Angela in a hushed tone, "just a little white trash."

Pretty and intelligent, Sonya Eden now dyes her hair black, sports a punkish pageboy haircut, and wears vintage clothes for her job at a museum. But the senior portrait from her high school yearbook reveals that this daughter of a high school biology teacher and an accountant had frizzy brown hair. Sonya herself jokes, "I was totally clueless." For Sonya, the toughest part of life at the University of Iowa was not the rigorous academic curriculum but the social interactions replete with hidden norms and mores. "There were two girls down the hall that smoked a lot of pot. And I walk in and I'm like, 'What is that?' You know, I didn't know, and my roommate just starts laughing and she's like, 'You don't know what that is?' I was like, 'No, what is that?' She's like, 'Sonya, it's marijuana.'" What Sonya said next made the awkward situation even worse. She yelled out: "Oh my God, they're smoking marijuana in *my* dorm room!" By revealing her shock and fear, Sonya was branded as the floor's official hick—a reputation from which she struggled to free herself for the next few years.

To the Achievers on track to cross state lines after graduation, college thus offers a test in adaptability to the social world beyond Ellis. Although it isn't an accurate microcosm of the real world, college does offer a chance for Ellis kids to decide if they want to shed their small-town skin and forge a new existence far from the gravel roads and cornfields of their youth. Along with the awkward and occasionally traumatic transitions, Leavers also experienced a thrilling sort of liberation in reinventing themselves while encountering a world that they had only read about in Mr. Ulrich's social studies class. They found freedom that would be impossible in Ellis. Although some young people returned home, judging this brave new world to be alienating, frightening, and mean-spirited, others stayed away because they hungered for more.

Being at college was "a little crack [opening] the door on a world," says Shannon Magnusson, a graduate student in physical therapy who was a three-sport athlete in high school and whose father grew corn before he sold his farm. "I think I needed to get out of the box. I led a very sheltered life, and when I went to college I was like, 'whoa.' . . . I needed college to see the world in a different light, and I needed to be a participant in the world. . . . You know, different everything, different culture, and starting out on my own. I really needed that freedom to experiment and try things without having people to identify me as what I used to be."

For Rose Rolland, her experiences in Iowa City, just one hundred miles from Ellis, would be a way station on a road that led out of the state for good. "Even though it was the middle of Iowa, it showed me that there was more to the world. This was the first time I had had minorities as friends. . . . I had never had a conversation or been friends with anyone who wasn't exactly like me." For the kids who make it beyond Ellis, their excitement at the prospect of difference and encounters with the exotic Other is a strong indicator they will not be coming home. For the first time, people they have never known, people who do not look, sound, or act like them—who are not white, Christian, or American—are living and breathing parts of their lives. Jerry Langtry, a University of Iowa student earning a teaching degree, told us how he's "had black roommates and [racially] mixed roommates, and it opens your eyes to how naïve you really are" about larger issues of privilege as well as smaller questions "like about how [African Americans] do their hair . . . just little things like that . . . the way people [have] different holidays, different religions." He added with a laugh that maybe the biggest change for him was coming to understand that not everybody is Lutheran.

Carl Garraway, an engineer who studied at the University of Iowa and who now lives and works in Chicago, also rates encountering diversity as one of his most significant life-altering changes after leaving Ellis: "Getting more exposure to different things, different types of people, different classes of people . . . racial and ethnic groups . . . I think that's been a great education in and of itself." Carl contrasts his experience at school with the often parochial views of his friends and family back home. "If my mom heard [me say I would never move back] she'd be like, 'Why?' With no disrespect, there is a level of ignorance among the people [back in Ellis]. It's possibly because they haven't been exposed to different situations in life that are presented to individuals in larger areas. . . . It's not very diverse. I'm sure it's 99 percent white, and that's uncomfortable for me. . . . You know, my job deals with multicultural people. . . . No disrespect to the people [in Ellis] or my family . . . It's too small, bottom line."

Jack Pederson, the law student mentioned at the start of the chapter, understands the price that must be paid for a big-city transformation. He is the first to admit that attending college has changed everything from his taste in clothes and food to the way he speaks and what he wants out of the world. Growing up in Ellis, he assumed he would be married by age twenty-one like the guys he saw at the local bar. Now, he observes, there is so much more he wants to do in life; getting married and starting a family have slipped to the bottom of his private list of priorities. These days, when Jack returns home, he needs time to acclimate to small-town life. He and his friends from Ellis who now attend universities have all noticed that they have a dual identity that manifests itself in their wardrobes. When they go home, they wear what Jack calls their "Ellis clothes": blue jeans, rock T-shirts, hooded sweatshirts—just the plain ones, not the kinds with the university logos on them—and non-brand-name sneakers or boots. As Jack explains, you can't go home and hang out at the bar and play pool wearing the clothes you'd wear to a bar on the Gold Coast. Such displays make it seem as if you've forgotten where you've come from and imply that you're looking down on the people who have remained close to home. "I don't want to come back seeming different than what I was when I left, [but] I think I have changed."

The experience of going off to college isolates the Achievers in myriad ways, but paradoxically, it also eases their transition to a new life far beyond the town where they grew up. Perhaps most important, the Achievers come to see leaving—and the metamorphosis that accompanies it—as disrespecting where you come from. The Style Network's reality show *How Do I Look?* captured this dilemma in an episode featuring a young Iowa woman with a degree from Duke who'd recently settled in Los Angeles. In the segment, billed as *"Little House on the Prairie* becomes *Sex and the City,"* we watched as the "recovering Iowan's" mousy hairstyle, flannel shirts, and blue jeans change into honey highlights and couture fashion. At the end of the show, she practices walking with high heels, and the host, Finola Hughes, declares that the last remnants of being a country bumpkin have been exorcised from the young woman's closet. We are told that the Iowa transplant, armed with her new look, is ready for her new life, her new career, and her search for "the right kind of man."

The show offered a staged and surreal version of the extreme makeovers that many Achievers undertake. Rushing the process of creating a new "look"—and, by extension, a new life—can result in an out-of-body excursion into vulnerability more akin to kids playing dress-up than to confident young people forging new trails. Whether the transformation takes shape through clothes, music, consumption patterns, new friends, or a love for travel, there is something intense about the changes that come with leaving. Some find that the trick to coping with these changes is striking a delicate balance between the person they're meant to be and where they come from.

The young people who leave Ellis to do great things someplace else must embrace how they are set apart. Ella Frankel, the young theology student we met earlier, spoke evocatively of her journey since high school and how this transformative experience imbued her leaving home with a sense of purpose and meaning. Had she not gone off to college, she said, "I would be such a different person than I am. I needed to experience a lot more than high school to become who I could be and to continue to develop and grow into the person that I believe I'm called to be." But Ella also struggles with the guilt of leaving people behind who did not benefit from the town's special investment. She reconciles this conflict by suggesting that some people are "equipped" to leave and others are not.

Even though she knows that earning a community college degree, getting married, and staying in Ellis were not for her, "that's not necessarily how it is or how it is supposed to be for other people. There are people who can be happy with whatever life [gives them], even with just a high school education." What marks the Achievers is that they won't be happy "making do" with a life in Ellis; they are restless, ambitious, and willing to trade in what they know for a chance at something more.

THE COSTS OF LEAVING

We found that, generally, Achievers don't second-guess their decisions to leave. The typical story does include a period of adjustment and homesickness, but with time this leads the Achiever to abandon her small-town traits and master a new set of orientations and expectations. New friendships and responsibilities push away old lives and connections. Once the hardest part about building a new life is over, the next move, from college campus to a bigger city, no longer feels so scary or momentous.

Elaine Weschler still remembers the pang of regret she felt when she left home for the first time. She started out at one of the smaller regional public schools, the University of Northern Iowa, but when things didn't go well for her there, she moved on to the University of Nebraska, where her boyfriend was studying. The couple wed two years later. During her first few months at a large university, her life seemed to her a disaster. She was miserable; at night, she wept over not seeing her family. She confided to her mother how disappointed she was, and her mother responded, "Well, you can't come back." For Elaine's mother, it was important that her daughter's life be bigger and more varied than what Ellis could offer. Elaine did harbor thoughts of returning to Ellis to raise children, but she knew this would signal failure to her family. In hindsight, Elaine declares that her mother was right. Settled and comfortable in Omaha—working at a bank, finishing her degree, and doing well financially—the likelihood of moving back to Ellis seems increasingly remote. Deep down, Elaine understands how much she has changed.

When Achievers who have made a life away from Ellis confront the fact that they probably will never return, they're almost wistful. Jonathan, the senator's aide living in D.C., sighs before saying that if he were to move back to the Midwest, "I doubt that I would go back to Ellis." He could see himself in Minneapolis, which is only about four hours from Ellis—that "wouldn't be out of the question"—but it would be tremendously difficult to entice him back to Ellis now that he has a taste for life in the big city. More important, the changes he recognizes in himself make him doubt he could readapt to small-town life.

THE PARADOX OF PREPARATION

A conundrum lies at the heart of the rural brain drain. Small towns are especially good at recognizing, nurturing, and launching talented individuals. They rally to prepare Achievers to leave, succeed brilliantly in doing so, then lament the loss of their combined talents. The adults of Ellis aren't ignorant of the paradox that traps them into expending resources to ensure that their most privileged, and in some ways most promising, young people leave. The challenge is getting these adults to imagine a different way of doing things.

Though the cultivation by family, teachers, and the wider community is crucial for many Achievers, if it ceased to happen tomorrow, talented young people would still strive to succeed in the wider world. Achievers are not merely propelled by the wishes of well-intentioned adults; in most cases they are determined to succeed for themselves, and they feel that to do so, they must go where there are more opportunities. In a certain way, then, there is an inevitability about how the Achievers' lives unfold. "It's just something drawing me out of the state, and I don't know what it is. It's not Ellis's fault, it's not Iowa's fault. It's just not for me, so I'm on my way out. That's all I can say" is how Jack Pederson, the young attorney, explained it.[12]

Any attempt to plug up the rural brain-drain and rebuild small towns must first acknowledge the basic truths of the process. Small towns invest far too heavily in the young people who are most likely to leave and who, once they build a new life elsewhere, are unlikely to return to Ellis for anything but an occasional visit. Abandoning the sifting and sorting system might seem to deny a fundamental mission of schools and communities to provide young people with the best possible start in life. But the reality is that the current system relies on an unequal and profoundly illogical allocation of resources that produces self-defeating outcomes for young people and the community as a whole. The time has come for towns like Ellis to reimagine, radically, what is best for their young people and their community. If they don't, the harsh truth is that these towns will, with time, simply disappear. The process has already started.

TWO

The Stayers

When you come from Des Moines you either accept
the fact without question and settle down with a girl
called Bobbie and get a job in the Firestone factory and
live there forever and ever or you spend your adolescence
moaning at length about what a dump it is and how you
can't wait to get out and then you settle down with a local
girl named Bobbie and get a job in the Firestone factory and
live there forever and ever.

—Bill Bryson, The Lost Continent

THE SMALL-TOWN IOWA OF SIXTY YEARS AGO, the one Lee Ulrich knew growing up, hardly resembles the town where he was reelected mayor in November 2007. Everything from the mom-and-pop stores on the old Main Street to the family farms that defined the pattern of the countryside have disappeared, devoured by megamalls, megafarms, and factories where robotic systems perform the tasks once assigned to human beings. Iowa still produces more eggs, hogs, and corn than any state in the Union and more than a few countries in the world; it's just that these goods come from a shrinking labor force overseeing "hog hotels" or a ten-thousand-acre spread of genetically modified crops. Ulrich believes that if one of the town's factories were to close, it would be a kick in the gut that would knock the town down so hard that it might never get back up. Over beers at Sally's, Ulrich confesses how he can't stop worrying. "You know," he says, talking into his beer bottle so that the men at the bar don't hear him, "we might not make it another five years. I think about that a lot."

Before Ulrich became Ellis's mayor, he taught history and social studies at the now-defunct Ellis Community Junior and Senior High School. As he lectured about current events and the Great Depression, if his students dared ask what grade he would be "giving" them for the term, Ulrich would correct them in his booming baritone: "I will never give you a grade. Like everything else in this life, it's just another thing you will have to earn." That lesson, Ulrich insists, was tailor-made for the kids who struggled most in his classes, the ones not headed to college who complained continually about how they would never need to do research papers with footnotes in "the real world." Teaching history was beside the point, Ulrich told us: "I didn't expect them to grow up and become historians." Ulrich would tell his charges that he was getting them ready to deal with "a life filled with struggle." In exchange for their coming to class on time and ready to learn, he would show his students how to be decent, hardworking citizens who contributed to society.

When Ulrich retired from the classroom, not long after he was sworn in as mayor for the first time more than a decade ago, he carried with him an up-close understanding of how a social engine pushed certain kids to leave and kept the rest close to home. He also could see, with absolute clarity, how the loss of so many young people, combined with the constraints trapping modestly educated young workers in the countryside, posed the greatest challenge to Ellis's viability for the next century. Back when he was a teacher, Ulrich struggled to get his colleagues to see how their overinvestment in the young people who leave was draining resources away from the ones who stayed—representing a crucial, missed opportunity. "It was as if all they cared about were the ones who were the first chair in the orchestra or playing varsity basketball," he said. Though he recognized the danger in writing off the local kids who remain close—the Stayers—even Ulrich struggled against the intoxicating appeal of focusing his time and energy on the most attentive and highly diligent students. All teachers want to bask in the accomplishments of students who work far beyond their grade level. No one enjoys standing in front of a classroom of knuckleheads who show up for class without books and a pencil.

During his years as a teacher, Ulrich had no qualms about calling out the troublemakers. He would make them look him straight in the eye and warn them that if they were just going to take up space in his classroom, maybe they were wasting everyone's time and shouldn't bother showing up at all. Sometimes, those wild, angry teenagers who marched out of his office in a thick fog of rage would return, promising to work harder and do better. In the years to come, one of Ulrich's greatest joys would be running into his former students, the ones who had become upstanding citizens with jobs at the plant or in construction and had families of their own. Sometimes they would tell Ulrich how much they appreciated the fact that he "never took their shit." Others felt differently. Some accused Ulrich of being the worst sort of teacher, someone who bullied his students and cared most about the kids who took their seats at the head of the class, the students with the right last names.

Ulrich is a true believer in the power of the American meritocracy to reward hard work and diligence; he never thought it was his place to debate the fairness of pushing some kids to go and others to stay. To him, trying to dismantle the sifting and sorting system makes about as much sense as informing the government that you've decided not to pay your taxes. What Ulrich recognizes is that the town's future rests in the hands of the young people who, in previous generations, supported themselves on family farms, working for the railroad or on a line. Ulrich remains convinced that to survive, Ellis needs the region's plants and some version of the farming economy, and so, as a teacher and, later, as a mayor, he has devoted himself to making sure the kids who remain have something to hold on to. Ulrich's greatest fear is that he may have betrayed those young men and women he taught for so many years, the ones he promised would be just fine if they worked hard, played by the rules, and never complained. Looking at the world the young people of his community will inherit, Ulrich now wonders if he taught them to believe in something that no longer exists.

If you travel around the Heartland, you'll encounter many isolated places where a lingering sadness hangs in the air: hundreds of miles away from the nearest city, the world surrounding Ellis orbits around this speck on the map at dizzying speed.[1] Here, kids still drag race on dusty country roads in a local practice known as gravel traveling. Boys holler at the girls, dressed in their cutest jeans, who spend an hour buying Cokes at Pronto's gas station and convenience store. The residents, especially the young ones, feel trapped in time.

For small-town kids, having access to a car is akin to breathing. But there are important differences in status. The Stayers tool around town in beat-up jalopies they buy and maintain themselves, whereas Achievers drive newer, nicer models. The "Snob Hill" kids and the town kids host parties in their parents' basement family rooms and watch movies, but the Stayers' socializing usually consists of drinking beers away from the view of the deputies. Their parties are at "the pits," an abandoned quarry right off Route 20, and when there isn't snow on the ground, they try to spin out perfect donuts on the empty highways. For many kids in the Heartland, NASCAR is more popular than the NBA, so when poor teenage boys in Ellis dream of making it big, they fantasize about racing in the Daytona 500. One of the most famous chroniclers of coming-of-age among small-town kids, H. G. Bissinger, writes, "Across the country there are thousands of towns just like it . . . places that had gone through the growing pains of America without anyone paying attention, places that exist as islands unto themselves."[2]

Most Stayers with whom we spoke knew where they were headed by the time they reached junior year. They say that in school, it was easy to tell the future Stayers from the Leavers, simply by the way they dressed. Stayers came to school wearing hand-me-down clothes, work boots, T-shirts, and the kinds of blue jeans and sneakers sold at the discount stores in Waterloo. If they had to milk cows or feed hogs at the crack of dawn, the stench hung over them even if they took a shower afterward and scrubbed themselves raw and red with the strongest deodorant soap. Their class rank and position in the school's pecking order reminded them daily that they were not like the Achievers.

Forty percent of Ellis High's entering freshman class will never set foot on a college campus nor live anywhere but Liberty County. If they are fortunate, they will find work at Safeguard, an ambulance manufacturer owned by Amos and Ralph Leinhardt; John Deere in Waterloo; or Tantech, a Cedar Rapids–based microprocessor-assembling firm, where full-time employees might earn $15 an hour after a year or two. Or they might make half as much at the meat-processing plants, egg factory, or cardboard-box factory, working alongside undocumented workers from El Salvador and Mexico.[3]

Steven Hennes, the manager of a dairy farm, is a taciturn twenty-eight-year-old with angular features who has never lived more than five miles from his parents' farm. Back in high school, no one would likely have seen much academic potential in him; when we wonder about his class rank, Steven responds, spitting out his chewing tobacco for effect, "I was about as low as you could get." Casey Annis is a brawny, chain-smoking twenty-five-year-old who supports his wife and three kids as a welder at Deere in Waterloo. He says that during high school, "I never did band or sports or anything like that." Such pursuits were the domains of the kids from Snob Hill, the ones who would move away right after graduation. Casey explains, "I was a work type." Peter Garton, a stocky, baby-faced thirty-year-old who never finished high school and now works on the killing floor at Con-Agra, says he and his high school friends were "the low-life type of people in the school who didn't really care about a lot of things." Henry Randall, a thirty-year-old truck driver, recently moved back home with his parents because his ex-girlfriend, the mother of his newborn son, took out a restraining order against him. Henry never finished high school, and, like most dropouts from Ellis, he never ventured far from home, except when he was on the road driving a semi, sleeping in the back of his cab. As Henry explains, there was a pretty clear social hierarchy when he was a student at Ellis High School: "You had your smart kids, your medium kids, and then you had your low kids." Stayers like him "were way below the low kids."

CAUGHT BETWEEN A ROCK AND HARD PLACE

In an irony not lost on the young people who would grow up to stay, the same teachers who inspired the town's best kids to dream of a life far beyond the countryside told the Stayers they would never amount to enough to get out of Ellis. The fact that young people rarely rebelled against the assumption that they would inherit their parents' place in the world demonstrates how powerful and all-encompassing the tendency toward social reproduction[4] could be; indeed, like the old adage says, the exceptions prove the rule. Jacob Rippentorp, age thirty, remembers how he worked hard to become an exception.

Less than six feet tall but fit and more than a little imposing, Jacob looks like a police officer even when he's dressed in a sweatshirt and baseball cap. Back in high school, Jacob says he was an average student who didn't participate in after-school activities and whose family was not one of the local elite. Because of these characteristics, Jacob says, he found himself set onto—from his view, shoved down—the Stayer path. "We had to take these aptitude tests back in high school. . . . The counselor told me, to my face, I shouldn't go to college. I should probably get a job in the factory . . . because I wouldn't make it." And yet Jacob did not go to work at Deere or Safeguard. He put himself through college, earning a degree in criminal justice. He lives and works in a Chicago suburb as a police officer. But for every young person like Jacob who resisted, far more young people followed the course set by the adults who supposedly knew better. Though it failed in Jacob's case, this steering could be overt and crude, and in many cases, it dovetailed seamlessly with the decisions that young people appeared to make of their own volition.[5]

Understanding how the Stayers choose and, at the same time, get chosen to remain is like listening to an old, sad hymn. Many scholars puzzle over why schools fail to operate as the meritocracies most Americans believe them to be. The Stayers may have attended a rural school in one of the more remote corners of America during the 1990s, but their stories bear a striking resemblance to the working-class boys the sociologist Paul Willis encounters in a 1970s industrial city in the British Midlands or to the group of friends growing up in a Boston housing project that a Harvard student named Jay MacLeod wrote about in the mid-1980s who failed in school because education had failed them.[6] The desire to go to college may be the defining aspiration for the Achievers, but for the Stayers, like so many working- and lower-class kids whose family incomes put them in the bottom quarter of the in-

come distribution, just surviving high school feels like a major ac-
complishment.

In some ways, rural dropouts are not very different from their
suburban and inner-city peers: typically, they earned lower grades,
scored poorly on standardized achievement tests, showed signs of
low self-esteem, and lacked a sense of control over their own lives.
More often than not, rural dropouts defend their decision to walk
away from education with the assertion that "school was not for
me."[7] Kids in the suburbs and cities make similar claims, and indeed, no matter where dropouts live, school sets the stage for future
economic prospects. And yet, in one of the many self-deceptions
implicit in how class patterns reproduce themselves generation after generation, the Stayers insist they choose their paths for themselves. At the same time, rural dropouts differ, crucially, in how
they rank work. Research on rural youths shows that their parents
are more likely to encourage their offspring to get full-time jobs,
attend trade schools, or enter the military rather than attend college; indeed, these "leveled aspirations"[8] extend to money. Rural
youth have parents who reject the American ethos of earning lots of
money and, instead, value making a good income, having a secure
job rather than a high-powered one, and holding onto friendships
as far more important priorities.[9]

Given how diligently the Stayers applied themselves to work,
how poorly they fared in school, and the fact that their parents
were not totally convinced of the need for college and careers, it is
easy to see how they abandoned higher education. College would
be nice, but trade school, a job at the plant, or a military tour were
just as good—and probably better, since they didn't cost so much.[10]
Peter Garton told a typical story: at age seventeen, he could take
home $200 a week working construction—earning as much as men
a decade older. That made it easy to decide that he had outgrown
education: "I just thought I had more important things to do than

school." So while the Achievers, focusing on their studies and extracurricular activities, assiduously avoided work, the Stayers ran as fast as they could to get it. This choice is pivotal for marking young people—like Marie Huss, a single mother who, at twenty-five, still gets carded when she goes out dancing with her girlfriends at their favorite country music bar in Cedar Falls—as Stayers.

Marie has never lived anywhere but Ellis, and she started finding the means to pay her way in the world by the age of twelve. Marie's parents were farmers with five kids, and they expected her to spend the money she earned babysitting to buy all her own wardrobe for school. By sixteen, she was working thirty hours a week at the local nursing home to get money for her car and insurance. Her job left her no time for homework, much less sports or other extracurricular activities that could matter for getting into college. Those long hours at her job made it possible to afford "a really nice car with a really high payment" and "cool clothes." Working, she believes, provided her with purpose, maturity, and direction. Marie recalls with pride, "I took care of people who couldn't take care of themselves and made sure they were healthy and made sure they were eating and bathed and dressed them and did all that. And to me, I thought that was a pretty grown-up job, so I felt pretty grown up at the time, and I had a lot of freedom." As work started to overtake her commitment to school, neither Marie nor her parents seemed very concerned, even when she went from being an honor student to just getting by with her grades. Why did she have to go to college and wait four more years for a good job when, as a teenager, she had already done so much? So what if her teachers did not see her accomplishments? Truth be told, the teachers at school didn't pay her much attention anymore. Marie never got in trouble, and she was not flunking out, but increasingly school was just the place where she spent time between work and home.

The decisions that Stayers consciously and unconsciously make in valuing work over education are easy to understand when one weighs the immediate gratification of having one's own money against the vaguer possibilities of what a degree and a career might mean for the future. What Marie didn't see back in high school was that eight years later, she would take home just a few dollars more an hour than she did as a teenager. Her paycheck—with the responsibilities of raising a child, as she has done since the age of nineteen—has meant that even with her full-time job, she finds herself eligible for welfare and food stamps.

It is not simply that the Stayers' parents didn't care about school. In a perfect world, the Stayers' parents indulgently daydream about their kids, who seem at first to have all sorts of untapped potential. But by the time they get to fifth, sixth, or seventh grade, and certainly when they enter high school, their grades and teacher reports are the cold, hard slap in the face to that earlier, intact optimism. Of course, the Stayers' parents would agree that attending college and becoming a doctor are better than having to break your back to survive, but for kids from the countryside, not earning a degree, or not having a profession, or starting a family at eighteen were hardly the end of the world. According to Steven Hennes, the dairy farmer, the only advice his parents offered was to "get some schooling and try to do what you can to get by with what you have." Steven watched his parents get through life without a diploma, and they taught their children how to work and take responsibility for the choices, for better or worse, that they would make.

The Stayers were raised by moms and dads who hadn't gone to college themselves and had survived.[11] Besides, they believed, college and education change you: college graduates start talking and acting differently or, in more than a few cases, begin looking down on where they came from. Such observations contributed to an uneasiness toward schooling and its transformative influences. Given that the Stayers' parents found it easier to believe in work than in school, it shouldn't be surprising that they put up precious little resistance to the official assessments from teachers and guidance counselors predicting their kids' modest academic prospects. And so, when the Stayers, the children of truck drivers and factory workers, got pregnant in high school or failed to earn the grades, scores, or scholarships to get into college, it wasn't a crushing disappointment or even all that unexpected. Their parents reasoned that attending college and indulging in the freedom to delay entry into the "real world" were simply more luxuries that their kids would be denied.[12] As parents, raising kids does not require putting them into stasis until they embark on their real adult lives. Like most people in Ellis, the Stayers' parents are the descendants of the homesteaders who built America, and that grit and determination is still in them. Their faith in the American dream took root in the unexamined assumption that their kids would be okay, somehow.

Dave Klinger, twenty-nine, is a machinist. With movie-star good looks and a thoughtful nature, you wouldn't guess that at age sixteen he failed classes and left school after a fight with a teacher, or that at seventeen, the girl he had been dating got pregnant and he became a father. As soon as he got his driver's license, he started working at the nursing home thirty-five hours a week, making $7 an hour, which back then wasn't far off from a grown man's paycheck. As Dave's mother and father watched their son pulling long hours, earning his own money, paying for his own car, their inclination was to assume he was a man. Dave recalls how by his junior year, "My mom never forced me to do my homework and didn't even know if I was going to school. At the time I thought it was great, but, you know, looking back on it, I think [it was easy to get to the] point where I'd failed too many classes."

The clear disconnect in how his family and his teachers viewed

Dave's behavior sent the sort of mixed messages that steer kids off course. Dave's parents may have thought he was fine; his teachers disagreed. What the school staff saw was a lousy report card and chronic truancy and tardiness. From their perspective, Dave was a disappointment at best, a failure at worst. Things finally came to a head in a social studies class taught by Lee Ulrich. "I didn't like [Ulrich's] class. . . . I had to be at work, like I had five minutes from the class to get over to . . . the nursing home [three miles away]." Dave says that he could have done it, but it was convenient for him to skip the class because he had two study halls right before it. And then one time he didn't have his work done for social studies, and Ulrich took him into the hall and told him that he just shouldn't be wasting his or anybody else's time; he should just drop out. The incident was a turning point. It still amazes and wounds Dave that no one chased him down the hall and told him to go back to his seat. His mother, he says, "didn't try to keep me in school, and my dad was kind of a little bit [concerned], but he didn't really say much. I mean, nobody really tried very hard to keep me in school, so that's kind of how it happened." And what about Lee Ulrich? Even now, Dave can't get his head around why Ulrich worked so hard to push him into a corner with an ultimatum that day. "Now when I look back at it, I just can't believe he told me to . . . I just don't understand why." We asked Ulrich about the incident, not mentioning Dave by name but describing the events from Dave's account. He was silent for a while, then said, "I'm not sure which student you mean. There are a couple; those sorts of things happened." He had no further comment. Rural kids are far more likely than urban or suburban peers to leave school for economic pulls such as a job or personal reasons such as pregnancy, marriage, disability, illness, or, as we see in Dave's case, an inability to get along with teachers.[13]

Many of the Stayer kids grew up in working-class households where their parents sent the message, loud and clear, that if they wanted the toys of adolescence—namely, a car or clothes—they would have to buy them for themselves. Within farming communities, the tradition of young people working is cherished precisely because it instructs them in the value of a dollar. But, truthfully, the more central concern was that in the households where the prices of milk, corn, hogs, groceries, and heating bills were a constant topic of conversation, the extra income that high schoolers brought home made it possible for families to get by from month to month. In contrast, the Achievers' parents, as we heard in the previous chapter, kept their kids from taking after-school jobs because they understood that grades and extracurricular activities mattered more. Either the Achievers' families made enough money to buy the accessories of adolescence for their offspring, or they made sacrifices, such as taking on side jobs, so their kids could devote themselves fully to academic pursuits.

As we've seen, Stayers do not drift off course in school without the complicity of adults. When they skipped class, no one came looking for them, and when they didn't turn in their homework, their parents shrugged their shoulders and told them to find a job. Teachers, staff, and parents may be indicted for dismissing the Stayers as rebellious, lazy, or just indifferent to school, thus dooming them to their limited prospects in the region's dying economy. Yet, it is also true that the Stayers damage their own futures when they preemptively reject school before it can reject them. Stayers were puzzled that their teachers viewed them as lazy, even though they worked twenty or thirty hours a week.

Stayers didn't just decide one day that school wasn't worth their time and effort. For the lesson to stick, they had to hear it repeatedly. Even though most Stayers did not cooperate in school, they managed to internalize the judgments from teachers who told them college wasn't for them. Stayers came to view their preference for work over school as just as legitimate and honorable as the pursuits of academically driven Achievers. The tragedy is that Stayers are blind to the reality of blue-collar work in a postindustrial economy. Their downfall is hubris, forged in their unwavering belief in the work ethic. At seventeen, they just could not see how their physical strength and willingness to work hard could ever betray them.

In another time, the Midwest was populated with company towns and local aristocracies in the form of entrepreneurs who made factories rise out of the prairie. Muncie, Indiana, had the Balls, five brothers who invented the home-canning jar, and Newton, Iowa, has the Maytags.[14] Technically, Ellis is no company town; no single entity employs most people there. But in recent years, some of the best blue-collar jobs for young people who aren't headed for college or the military can be found at Safeguard.

When the Leinhardts arrived in Ellis about fifteen years ago, they didn't have a big, established company in the process of expanding production; rather, they were a start-up family business eager to spread its wings. Amos Leinhardt's father, Morris, had grown up in a rural North Dakota community very much like Ellis, so he understood what bringing one hundred factory jobs to this town would mean. For its part, the Ellis business community used all the incentives at its disposal to woo Safeguard: generous financing, a deal on the property, and more than a few drinks at Sally's. So when Amos Leinhardt purchased the late Doc Stillworth's house and moved his family to town to oversee daily operations, the Leinhardts hitched their fate to Ellis.

From the Leinhardts' perspective, the town and its inhabitants made them prosper. Fortunately for Ellis, they were not the type of businesspeople who would move their manufacturing overseas just to drive up profit margins. Four years ago, when Morris's declining health pushed father and son to look to the future, the Leinhardts acted against their own best interests, choosing not to sell the company in a public offering. Instead, they arranged for Safeguard to be purchased by their own employees. By doing so, they lost 10 to 15 percent of the money they could have gotten if they'd sold to outside stockholders—a noble act that totally violates the dominant credo of today's "it's nothing personal, it's just business" corporate world. But for self-described "small-town people" like the Leinhardts, their success far exceeded their wildest expectations. Safeguard is called the Cadillac of ambulances. As legend has it, when Dale Earnhardt crashed at Daytona in 2001, it was an ambulance built in Ellis that transported the mortally injured racing star. The Leinhardts believed they owed Ellis for their success, and if they couldn't afford to fund a university or endow a park, at least they wouldn't be the ones to stab the town in the back.

Precisely because the company employs the men and women who are not in a position to leave Ellis, Ulrich believes, "Safeguard is the knight on a white horse that saved an entire generation of the town's workers." Amos Leinhardt disagrees with this rosy assessment; Safeguard's being open won't change the fact that stores such as Wal-Mart are nothing more than "Main Street killers," that people don't do their shopping at the town's hardware and grocery stores, or that even with all the old folks living in town and at the nursing home there isn't enough business for Ellis to sustain its pharmacy. There's no way a single plant with one hundred people building ambulances in a flyover corner of Iowa can be any more stable than the billion-dollar multinationals such as Maytag, Whirlpool, or Winnebago. The company could go belly-up anytime: though it is unlikely, the workers themselves might decide to cut and run, take their money, and watch the ambulances get built in Mexico. Even if the workers own Safeguard and the jobs at Deere in Waterloo are safe, Leinhardt knows that Ellis is just treading water: "This town is just surviving, but what we really need is to grow."

Only occasionally does the Heartland make the evening news, and unfortunately the only time the people who truly have the power to stabilize America's Heartland pay attention to towns like Ellis seems to be during presidential campaigns. This is when politicians fight for the votes of salt-of-the-earth blue-collar types in contested purple states such as Iowa, Pennsylvania, and Ohio— where the manufacturing sector is the canary in the coal mine, warning the nation that economic downturns and unemployment are heading their way soon.[15] The general trend toward deindustrialization has gathered speed as NAFTA and the recession of 2001 severely depleted the manufacturing base of many Midwestern states. Tellingly, the top candidates for the Democratic nomination in 2008, Barack Obama and Hillary Clinton, were quick to criticize free-trade agreements and rewards for firms that outsource jobs.[16] Yet many economists point out that the erosion of jobs may have more to do with global economic ebbs and flows than with regional trade agreements.[17] The twenty-first-century high-growth sectors fueled by financial services and bio- and high-tech were not economies that would benefit those modestly educated workers whose fortunes had risen during the heyday of American manufacturing nearly fifty years ago. To the young people who stayed in the countryside, it felt as if the rural crisis had come in the middle of the night while they slept. Long before the bosses mailed out a thousand pink slips, the rural economy would suffer a slow, torturous death by a thousand cuts: cuts in pay, cuts in health insurance and pension plans, cuts in work hours, cuts in new hires, cuts in full-time workers, and, of course, the farcical negotiations in which the beaten, bloodied labor representatives declare a Pyrrhic victory just for staving off closure for another year.

"WORK WAS SOMETHING I WAS RAISED TO DO"

Life in a farming community teaches the value of hard work. From a very early age, kids who grow up working alongside the adults in their family come to understand that their efforts matter for a successful harvest and getting the farm through another year. In the pantheon of categories that exist at Ellis High, there were jocks, band and theater geeks, teachers' pets, nerds, and the kids who worked.

In the summer months, local kids, along with some of the town kids who were saving for college, worked on farms detassling corn, walking the beans, and picking rock. Each of these painstaking jobs is vital to a successful growing season. Picking rock is a crucial step for seasonal harvesting; all the rocks and pieces of debris must be cleared from the fields so the machinery can get through unhindered. Walking the beans is necessary because most Iowa farmers rotate their crops, alternating between corn one year and soybeans the next. Armed with a cutting blade, workers walk between rows of soybeans and cut out the volunteer corn and other weeds that may have been missed by the cultivator. Detassling corn means removing the seed tassels to prevent carefully engineered hybrid feed corns from cross-pollinating. When our young Iowans came of age in the late 1980s and early 1990s, it was common to see yellow school-bus loads of teenagers from all over the county working in the fields.[18] A local high school wrestling coach even organized his own crew; he probably figured picking rock was a good way to condition his team and for them to make a little money on the side.

Because of the extreme summer conditions, a farmhand's tasks start at dawn and end in late afternoon. Despite the harsh physical demands, the lure for local teenagers was that as long as they could endure the heat, humidity, sun, and swarms of bugs, at the end of the summer they would be rewarded with enough cash for a new car or a year's worth of money to live on during high school. Some of the town kids worked alongside the country kids on their summer break because the jobs paid so well. The difference is that while the Leavers and the Stayers might pick rock or detassle corn together from June to August, once September came and school started, the sons and daughters of the teachers and lawyers devoted their after-school energy to their studies and sports, whereas their classmates not headed for college remained on as field hands for the harvest.

Kids growing up in the countryside are not segregated in the labor force the way kids in more densely populated metropolitan areas are. Being an hour's drive from the nearest mall means that teens from Ellis can't earn extra money selling scoops of gourmet ice cream or folding clothes at the Gap. Some of the Stayers collected their first paychecks employed as farmhands by the massive corporate agribusinesses, and many of the girls, and even a few boys, found jobs with the town's most reliable employer, Valley-crest Nursing Home, where, after completing a six-week certification course, anyone older than age sixteen could be certified as a nurse's aide. Many male Stayers' fathers worked in construction or fixed cars, and so, just as young men coming of age in rural America have done for generations, they learned their fathers' trades.

Stayers' introduction to the labor force and their intense, year-round participation in it starting as young teenagers fed their misplaced conviction that they would be able to get the sorts of blue-collar jobs that make someone middle class in America.[19] Before graduating from high school, the future Stayers would earn almost as much as the adults working alongside them. What they could not see was that under the rules of the new economy, these were the jobs that quickly maxed out in terms of earning potential or upward trajectory, so the jobs Stayers held at seventeen would hardly be different from the jobs they held at forty-seven. Earning $10 an hour and having no health insurance or pension can be a disaster when you reach thirty or forty, but at eighteen these circumstances feel very different. With money in your back pocket, your parents treat you as if you're a grown-up, allowing you to come and go as you please and make choices for yourself. Stayers say their parents never expected them to get rich, just to earn a decent income and pay the bills. Their parents could not grasp the grand sweeping transformations of postindustrial, post-Fordist capitalism and the long-term impact of stagnating wages that had trapped them. When they did start to make the connections and figured out what had happened, it was too late to warn their kids. If they couldn't save themselves, they didn't see how they could make their kids much better off.

After graduating from high school, Stephanie Cannell, a former cheerleader with long dark hair and sad eyes, wasn't motivated to follow her classmates to a community college. Her first job was as an assembler on the midnight–to–8 a.m. shift at Tantech, the same place her mother worked. When the company lost one of its contracts, as a part-time worker she was let go; cutting her hours didn't cost the company unemployment insurance. For the next year, Stephanie bounced around from one minimum-wage job to another: first at Burger King for $5.15 an hour, then at the local supermarket.[20] The money wasn't great, but it was enough to pay for her car, which she "couldn't really afford."

Stephanie got pregnant around this time, and her boyfriend, Todd, who worked construction, did not stay in the picture very long. When he left, he took his paycheck with him. Working a minimum-wage job, even when Todd was still around, made Stephanie eligible for welfare. After he left, things got even worse. Feeling desperate, Stephanie tried to find work at Tantech again. Her mother, June, who had worked the assembly line for ten years, stopped by Human Resources constantly to see if something new had opened up. June also started lobbying the shift supervisors directly on her daughter's behalf. Stephanie, now twenty-three, jokes that her mom, normally an unassuming, quiet woman, waged a full-frontal assault to get her daughter a job. "She would tell them, 'She's already worked here for a year, you had no problems with her, why not hire her back?'" Eventually, her nudging paid off, and Stephanie returned to Tantech after a scary year and a half. "My mom really wanted me to have a good job."

It's striking how much Stephanie's 8-a.m.-to-4-p.m. "mommy's hours" shift job as an assembler, which pays less than $9 an hour, transformed her life. Working at Tantech means that Stephanie and her son are protected from the indignities of public assistance and welfare workers, and she can count on a steady paycheck that will go a long way toward raising a family. But what if the plant had another round of layoffs, and she lost her job? This time, Stephanie wants to be prepared: she and her mom are going back to college through the company's tuition-benefits plan. Stephanie survived her first brush with the new economy, and she says she longs to get back to school so she doesn't get mired in the quicksand of minimum-wage work again. With any luck, we joke, the only time she will be in a Burger King is to get her son a Whopper Junior. Another contract lost and a turn in the economy, and Stephanie, a self-sufficient single mom with her own house and a decent job, could find herself back on welfare in a flash.[21]

Many of the Stayers don't fully comprehend the rules of the new economy until they get steamrolled by them. "Nowadays, everything is so much computers that either you are going to be a laborer or you're going to be on your butt behind a computer. You get to do one or the other. And if you're not good at reading or writing, like I am not, you'd better learn some alternatives," explains Casey

Annis, the welder who works alongside his parents at John Deere. After walking out of high school with a diploma and some money in their pockets, the Stayers believed that getting a job would deliver them from the petty exclusions of the world of high school. Why should they endure the indignities of not being the ones expected to accomplish anything when they believed they had more important things to do than school? But hindsight is twenty-twenty, and ten years later, the Stayers who sprinted to get out of school would find themselves looking back on their missteps. There is Stephanie Cannell, the single mother who survived welfare and is trying to figure out how to get a degree; Courtney Rillings, a convenience store clerk wistfully imagining what might have been if she had headed off to college; and David Klinger, who blames the adults who should have known better for not keeping him on track. A decade of working has shown them all that their parents and teachers were wrong; it wasn't a good idea to find work in the plant. Working hard and playing by the rules would not bring their own reward. Klinger has worked in full-time jobs since leaving high school at sixteen and hasn't gotten a raise in four years. His job could disappear, and there is almost no chance he could work anywhere else with better wages, better benefits, or more security. At twenty-five, Dave feels finished. "There's no ladder to climb."

"AROUND HERE, TWENTY-FOUR IS OLD TO BE GETTING MARRIED"

Leaving school and starting work are not the only things Stayers do faster. In every facet of their lives, Stayers settle in for the long haul far sooner than their college-bound Achiever peers.

Though the median age for first marriage in Iowa is twenty-four, just a year younger than the nation as a whole, for the Stayers—mostly young women who left Ellis only to take an accounting or medical-assistant class at a community college or never left Liberty County at all—marriage and children were things that happened, quite typically, around the age of twenty-one.[22] Though unusual, one young Ellis woman had sought a judge's permission to wed her husband at seventeen; another married her high school sweetheart at nineteen, when she discovered she was pregnant. In the laughing words of Sara Alfred, twenty-eight, a teacher who resisted pressure from family and friends who couldn't understand why she was waiting so long to marry the boyfriend she had dated since junior prom, "Around here, twenty-four is old to be getting married."

With all the talk of hooking up and party rape on college campuses, it's tempting to long for the days of dating high school sweethearts.[23] Looking at the Stayers' mating rituals is like discovering a time capsule from the 1950s, an era when the majority of Americans wed by the age of twenty-four, shotgun weddings hadn't gone out of style, and marriage was seen as more of an obligation than a preference.[24] Attending a four-year college builds natural delays for marriage, although going to college is hardly the only reason for postponing a wedding. Higher education and high-status careers, goals that are linked with the twenty-first-century experience of emerging adulthood, erode young people's preferences for marriage.

Courtney Rillings, a twenty-three-year-old wife and mother with cornflower blue eyes and straight brown hair that falls below her shoulders, talks with us after she's cleared away the dinner dishes. Courtney, who works at a convenience store, married at age nineteen, and was pregnant on her wedding day, believes that if she had followed her Achiever friends to college, she wouldn't be a wife and mother now. "I would've met other people. I would've wanted to be free and just have fun and do the whole free-spirit college thing." To her way of thinking, marrying young, as she has done, "is a small-town thing." After getting out of high school, couples decide to wed because "you figure, you guys have been together so long, and it's not gonna make a difference."

In a social milieu where testing out different partners and waiting to get married just doesn't happen, there is no existential crisis about being ready to make the ultimate commitment. Relationships that endure "for a certain amount of time" lead to marriage, effortlessly and inevitably. Laura Carpenter, a thirty-year-old housewife who wed at age nineteen, explains the process. "You know, I didn't think anything of it. I thought that's just what I had to do. Not that I had to do it, I just—that's what I wanted to do. I was at the point in my life where I was like, 'Let's get this going.'" Young people pursuing higher education find a variety of other priorities to occupy their time and energy, while in Ellis, marriage and childbearing seems to be at the top of a short list of things to do. Moreover, when faced with pregnancy, couples in the countryside are far more likely to respond with marriage than with cohabitation.[25]

So what is the trouble with these young couples following the traditional patterns of mid-twentieth-century life by marrying far earlier than their more affluent, educated, urban peers? Though the marriage traditionalists might celebrate the countryside as a throwback to a better time, the truth is that marriages before the age of twenty-three face a far greater chance of resulting in divorce within ten years. And this risk of divorce contributes to a greater risk for poverty, because single motherhood, whether it results from divorce or nonmarital childbearing, is the primary reason for economic insecurity among women and children.[26] If we take the state of marriage as a barometer of conditions in Iowa, the fact that marriage is becoming more breakable, and that more women and children are following the path into poverty long associated with distressed urban centers, suggests that trends witnessed in ghettoes have now spread to the countryside. And what does it mean if Iowa, traditionally one of the most married states in the Union, is no longer immune to the sorts of hardship and suffering that Americans only expected to find in the most troubled parts of Baltimore or Philadelphia?

SMALL-TOWN TROUBLES

In towns like Ellis, no kids are strangers. Most people are related to one another, if one goes back far enough, through either marriage or birth. Small-town schools set the rhythm of life there, and any young person seen tooling around town when school is in session catches people's attention. One young man recalled the time he tried, but failed, to cut class. Apparently, his car had given him away; someone in a house near the school spotted him pulling out of the parking lot after the bell rang. The deputy caught up with him just a few minutes later. "Yah," he explained to us, "they know which kids drive what cars." In places where people stay put for generations, it's just harder to get away with things.

But the greatest myth of small-town life is that nothing bad ever happens there. Rural kids have distressingly high rates of suicide,[27] early childbearing,[28] and alcohol abuse,[29] as high as anywhere else, and school shootings occur more frequently in isolated rural places.[30] It's not simply that kids coming of age in the countryside get in trouble; there are also important differences in how this trouble is viewed. When the Achievers missed class, they received excused absences, whereas the Stayers got detentions. Stayers speeding down Main Street were cited for a moving violation; when the Achievers did the same thing, the same deputy wished them luck in the big game. While the Stayers' parties got busted by police, the Achievers' drinking was considered harmless fun, a precursor to their social life on a college campus in a year or two.

When our young Iowans were growing up, their preferred drug

of choice was alcohol. During the late 1990s, a synthetic form of speed, whose typical users are white and rural, would change all that. With the spread of methamphetamine, this drug epidemic would unravel life in the countryside. Law-enforcement officials consider meth to be the fastest-growing drug threat in America. The Heartland's countryside, with its small police departments operating in isolation and its easy access to the ingredients, space, and tools required for the drug's manufacture, was the ideal location for the ascent of a new growth industry: meth capitalism. Across the nation, meth has more regular users than crack, and since 1994 meth use has nearly tripled.

By 1999, there were three hundred times more meth-lab seizures in Iowa than in New York and New Jersey combined, according to statistics from the Drug Enforcement Agency. Iowa has claimed some major victories: state and federal officials embarked on a successful campaign to restrict the sales of cold medicine with pseudoephedrine and called on agriculture retailers and farmers to place locks on fertilizer tanks with anhydrous ammonia, both key ingredients for meth production. Since every pound of meth produces six pounds of hazardous waste, curtailing the proliferation of the labs saved the state millions of dollars annually by reducing the need for costly lab cleanups. But making it difficult to cook meth in Iowa did nothing to reduce people's appetite for the drug. With the Beavis-and-Butthead–style meth-lab operations out of the way, the Mexican drug cartels moved in to take a bigger share of the market.

In 2007, more than one in one hundred Iowans older than age twelve reported using meth in the past year, ranking the state fifteenth in the nation for meth use. "Like crack, meth drives up all the other problems in these communities. Meth users tend to be erratic, violent, and, in some cases, borderline psychotic—especially when on a sleepless binge or 'tweaking' episode. Users abandon families, lose jobs, and batter spouses and loved ones."[31] The question of whether the spread of meth has something to do with the loss of good-paying jobs in small towns, observes the writer Timothy Egan, "is an echo of a question—the one posed about crack and heroin use in gutted inner cities."[32] Should we be more troubled by the fact that so few people seem to be connecting the dots between the rise of crack in the inner city and the spread of meth in the countryside?

The summer we lived in Ellis, the town's chief of police, Daryl Meyer, had grown quite accustomed to orchestrating massive drug raids—with helicopters, hazmat teams, and heavily armed federal agents driving SUVs with tinted windows—that resembled scenes from an action blockbuster. Local dentist Dennis Daugherty noticed that more and more of his younger patients had the blackened, rotting teeth known as "meth mouth," which is caused by the cracked teeth and grinding that is symptomatic of tweaking.[33] Over at the Ellis pharmacy, before it closed, Rob Hubler, the druggist, and his wife, Jan, who worked the counter, took note of which customers purchased unusually large amounts of Sudafed. Driving by abandoned farmhouses, neighbors would check to see if there were several cars and trucks parked in the driveway or strange odors emanating from the property.

Mike Craun, a handsome, soft-spoken new father who meets us at our house in Ellis, somehow doesn't fit his wild history. As a high school senior, Mike worked in construction, which made it possible for him to finance his partying lifestyle. His first employer—his father, Rich—counted on his son to keep the tiny family construction business afloat. How Mike and his friends spent their time off never prevented him from being industrious on the job during the day. Mike says his parents were worried about what he and his friends were doing but had little knowledge about how out of control things had become. Mike thinks they stood back because they thought he'd have to make his own mistakes and figure things out on his own. His family became aware of all that Mike was doing when he celebrated his twenty-first birthday.

After a week of hard partying, using so many drugs that he can't remember exactly what he did, who was there, or how long he went without eating or sleeping, Mike tried to drive home. He was out in the middle of an unincorporated section of Liberty County known as Smokeville to those involved in the meth scene. The isolated location was ideal for keeping activities hidden from curious neighbors. He drove his car off the road into a ditch. When he woke up, not sure if he'd been asleep or unconscious, he called a friend to come get him. Not realizing he was still tweaking, Mike remembers, "I didn't even know anything was wrong with me. I looked at my car, and you couldn't even recognize it." Somewhere between crashing his brand new car and calling his friend, Mike had set the car on fire. "I don't know why I did, but I took the plates off the car and threw them." His friend arrived and drove him to his parents' house. The Crauns had not seen their son for days, and they were shocked to see cuts on his face. Mike could have lied or left out some details, but for some reason he didn't. He told them about the farmhouse, Smokeville, crashing the car, waking up by the side of the road. Terrified and confused, his parents, not knowing what else to do, called the Ellis police. When the officers discovered the remains of the burned-out car, they half-expected there to be a corpse beside it. Mike was arrested for arson, but given his demeanor, the police and the judge decided to send him to a hospital. They feared Mike meant to kill himself.

"Why did you get into all this crazy stuff?" we ask. Mike answers, "I was just bored."[34]

Two years have passed since the birthday celebration, and Mike is back working now. While in the hospital, he met a pretty nurse's aide named Amy, who was eighteen. Unlike the party girls Mike had been with before, Amy was serious. Still in high school, she worked at the hospital because she wanted to go to community college and become a nurse. Mike and she started talking when he returned to the hospital for his outpatient follow-ups.

Since Amy came into his life, Mike tells us, "I haven't been doing any drugs or anything." Amy and Mike now live together, and she's finishing her nursing degree. They are engaged and have a one-year-old son named Dylan. No wedding date has been set, but they will marry after she gets her RN. Mike says he's "doing good." Finding Amy and becoming a father have been a calming influence. We wonder what would have happened to him if he hadn't crashed the car and set the whole chain of events in motion. Mike answers, "Not in prison, but [I'd] probably [be] in jail." There would be no Amy and baby Dylan, but, Mike adds, smiling, "I'd still have a really nice green race car."

His friends have not been so fortunate. Mike remembers how, after his own arrest, they just wouldn't listen to him. "I told them they were gonna get into trouble 'cause, I mean, you could [cook meth] in a big town, but in a small town like Ellis, everybody knows everything." Mike had heard warrants were coming; there was talk in town that law officers "were coming around talking to people, asking questions about why they were out driving around so late." Mike says, "I told them, you know, this is going to come down pretty soon. They just, I don't know, they were hooked on it or they didn't believe it or what." Mike had managed to keep a job while using meth in intense spurts, but his friends didn't work and were paying the bills, and feeding their habit, by cooking meth for themselves.

We met Mike in the summer of 2001, and it was in the previous January that people had started getting arrested. Mike would be called to testify about the use of drugs in town. One friend, the ringleader from a well-to-do family who was friendly with the chief of police, ended up in a federal boot camp. Another received a phone call warning him that the authorities were on their way and that he should pack his bags and leave town for good; he took the good advice. Most people in Ellis know he's up in Minnesota, and many know where he is, but people figure he's someone else's problem now.

WHY WOULD I WANT TO LEAVE?

Although, as we've discussed, economic and social forces keep certain kids in Ellis, the strongest hold over many of them is that they simply like the town. They're comfortable there and cannot really imagine living anywhere else. The lyrics of John Mellencamp's song "Small Town" ring true for many of our Stayers. When we asked them why they stuck around, their responses were shot through with a tinge of puzzled amusement; no one had ever asked before. As Mellencamp's verse so clearly states, this was the place they would be until they die.

The worst and best features of life in Ellis are that people know you, you never have to lock your doors, there is no traffic, and, although crimes occur, people sense that it's more difficult to get away with them here because no one is anonymous in a small town. For those who remain in Ellis, living in a place where people feel as if they know you as well as you know yourself and "there are no secrets" is a source of infinite comfort. For others, it could be a source of madness.

The Stayers don't long for change and adventure; they prefer, instead, to be surrounded by like-minded people. Such an inclination grates against the normative underpinnings of pluralism, in which diversity ought to be valued over homogeneity. The truth is, the majority of Americans inhabit highly segregated worlds, and the elites who claim to put such a high premium on tolerance pretend this social isolation is an accident, rather than a clear, willful act. In Ellis, there are no such pretensions. It's just common sense that people prefer to be around those who share their orientation to the world. And yes, it is safe to infer that being around people who are like you means that the Other will be tolerated but not necessarily accepted. The central dilemma of life in the countryside is that its inhabitants want to lock themselves away from the outside world, yet to sustain life in their remote corner they must let that world in.

The Stayers' wings get clipped around the time they start working in high school. Their lightning-fast entry into the labor force gives them cash in their pockets, but what they fail to realize is that short-term financial independence will not be enough when they are adults and have a mortgage, children, and a retirement to fund. Many of the young people who stay in the countryside get tripped up when they try to play by twentieth-century rules in a twenty-first-century economy, and by the time they do understand, it's too late.

It is remarkable how much the Stayers talk about the comfort and security of small-town life, given the growing uncertainty they face. Even with the grim shadow of meth and the spread of poverty and joblessness, people in Ellis cherish the fact that the chaos, insecurity, and danger they associate with the wider world is not found to the same degree in the countryside. Several Stayers described Ellis as a haven where their kids could run free, be safe, and practically raise themselves. And though most Stayers have seen little of the world beyond Liberty County, they know that the unguarded way they raise their children would be impossible in urban America. When we lived there for a summer as parents of a two-year-old daughter, we, too, were struck by the lack of fear in

Ellis compared to back home in Philadelphia. In our regular visits to the Ellis community swimming pool, we noted scores of unsupervised young children who biked alone to the pool each day and spent their time cavorting in and out of the water under the casual watch of teenage lifeguards. Very often, when we went to the pool with our daughter, Camille, our presence there doubled the number of adults watching over the children.

This enviably relaxed approach to child supervision was at odds with our own urban, middle-class experience, one in which children are raised and protected in a cocoon-like existence. But only a few of the town's middle-class denizens shared our surprise at the relative lack of supervision; overall, it was a socially accepted practice. For Stayers, living in a place where their children could grow up and play freely, as their parents had during their childhoods, consistently ranked among the top reasons for remaining there.

The social and economic context might overshadow the sort of lives Stayers lead, but it is important to see that even though they don't overanalyze their decisions and appear fairly content with their circumstances, they face a major challenge in their diminishing capacity, in the new economy, to sustain protected lives. The problem with the Stayers' choice of work and money over education is that they effectively close off one of the most reliable escape routes from the countryside—and their best chance at economic security. It also means that a disproportionate number of the workers who will determine the future of the Iowa labor force will be particularly ill suited to adapt to the economy's increasing demands for educational credentials and technical skills for all but the most basic of jobs.

Stayers are the harbingers of troubled times in the small towns of the Heartland. They are the people most likely to be poor, and they are victims of the Midwest's meth epidemic. They must also be a vital part of the solution to the hollowing-out problem. That they have been largely overlooked suggests that they are an as yet untapped resource, and this book's conclusion includes recommendations that can help small towns renew themselves and prepare for the challenges of an increasingly globalized and unpredictable future that is already transforming life in the rural Heartland.

THREE

The Seekers

I'm from Iowa originally. It took me a long time to
realize we were free to go. I was like twenty-one
before I was like . . . "We can just leave?"
— comedian Jake Johannsen

THE IOWA-BORN COMEDIAN JAKE JOHANNSEN, who tours
the nation on the stand-up circuit and lives in California, sums
up the Seeker experience and sensibility in this joke from his act.
Before Johannsen achieved success as a comic, he completed his
engineering degree at the University of Iowa. Lots of kids might
dream of leaving Iowa, but without college or the military as a catalyst, few of them ever do.

The eminently appealing story of the small-town kid exploring
the world on his or her own might seem like the more authentic
Seeker experience. The truth is, of the young people armed only
with a high school diploma who ever do manage to leave Iowa, precious few get very far without enlisting in the military first.

THE RECRUITER

Yesterday was the last day of the football season. Rows of helmets
sit neatly on the shelves, waiting to be packed away until next season. We meet Justin Engstrom, one of the team's graduating se-

niors, as he leaves the coach's office. With a tousled head of blond curls and wearing a worn, gray, hooded Fighting Cougar sweatshirt, Justin looks exactly the way one would picture a high school football player from the Midwest: lean and muscular, with a face still tanned from working outside all summer. This juxtaposition—a country boy's countenance with a grown man's bearing—offers a jarring reminder of why we are at the high school today. A National Guard recruiter is on his way to speak with Justin, and we will sit in on the conversation. Justin is eighteen, and like thousands of other kids from across the Heartland, he is thinking about going off to war.

Right on schedule, Corporal Allan Traylor, an Army National Guard recruiter for Liberty County, sticks his head around the main doorway of the high school's offices. The secretaries greet him by name and usher him into the principal's office, where he settles into the most comfortable chair at the conference table. School visits are part of Traylor's regular rounds. With an all-volunteer force during wartime, the pressure to find young people willing to enlist has never been higher.[1] And so recruiters like Traylor make weekly if not daily pilgrimages to the schools in their area; many will informally colonize space in the guidance center. A cross between salesmen and servicemen, recruiters bombard the school staff with requests for yearbooks, transcripts, and the inside scoop on students who might be inclined toward the armed forces. The military's manual for recruiters advises them to "become fixtures at the schools," to spend as much casual off-time with prospective enlistees as possible. There are also the frequent phone calls and heart-to-heart chats with students; many recruiters even attend school events, such as football games and wrestling meets. Recruiters are taught how to identify the popular kids—known in marketing terms as the "centers of influence"—and how to carefully orchestrate conversations with them in highly visible locations where many students can witness. A computer program called Blueprint tracks these interactions. After a student decides to enlist, recruiters offer advice on how to handle anxious parents' concerns. In reality, recruiters use the same techniques as admissions counselors from elite colleges. The difference is that for the military recruiters, high schools in working-class farm and factory towns throughout the nation's Heartland serve as their equivalent of "feeder schools."[2] Privileged kids hailing from the affluent public and tony private schools that operate a conveyor belt to the Ivy League will hardly ever see recruiters like Traylor.

On this crisp November day, in his conversation with Justin, it is Traylor who does most of the talking. This is not Justin's first meeting with a recruiter; he is still considering other options, including the Army, Marines, and Navy. Traylor follows a standard script designed to anticipate the potential recruit's questions: he proffers information about scholarships, he outlines the realities of boot camp, and, not surprisingly, he emphasizes the opportunities for travel and training that the Guard provides. He works hard to keep the tone upbeat and positive. This is no simple feat, given that in fewer than ten minutes, Traylor has the unenviable job of selling a kid like Justin on the allure of military life in the face of record-long deployments and accelerated combat rotations.

Even in this buyers' market, Justin offers the safe and expected answers. Eager to please and to make a good impression, he talks about the military as a tradition in his family: many of his relatives, including his uncles and a grandfather, have served. Growing up in Ellis, he'd "heard the stories" of seeing the world and going to battle, and he says he wants "to protect the country" in a time of war. But even with Justin's patriotic sentiments, most of his questions for Traylor have to do with the practical issues of training and tuition programs. Time in the military will ultimately help him to become an electrician, he says. But there seems to be more that Justin isn't saying—something vaguely perceptible beneath his formal politeness. Near the end of their meeting, Justin asks Traylor whether an arrest for a DWI a year ago will affect his eligibility to enlist. Although Justin seems genuinely worried and embarrassed, Corporal Traylor appears unfazed, and he confidently assures Justin that this previous arrest should not be a problem.

Later, when they finish their official appointment, we ask Justin what he thinks he'll accomplish by entering the military. Once again, Justin talks vaguely of serving his country and getting training. But we push him for a more complete explanation: "Step back and think in bigger terms about the risks you're taking. What will you, *Justin*, get out of enlisting?" He struggles for an answer, and after a long pause he announces: "I'm going to be a father. My girlfriend's pregnant, [and] the baby will be here in February." We congratulate him. But again, we point out, he still has not told us why he wants to enlist, and shouldn't a new baby make him want to stay close? Laughing sheepishly, Justin offers us a new, markedly different reason for enlisting: "the money." If Traylor is surprised by Justin's frankness, it doesn't show. "How much money will you get?" we ask Justin, but Traylor breaks in, responding as an automatic reflex. This is, after all, the question he hears from young people all over Iowa every day. "Twenty thousand dollars paid out over three years, and if he does his time serving in combat, 100 percent tuition at any school in the state of Iowa."

"Enlistment bonuses"[3] have become one of the recruiters' most powerful aids in helping make their targets. Steve Coll reports in the *New Yorker* that "to persuade soldiers and young officers" to enlist "after increasingly long combat tours, the Army's spending on retention bonuses increased almost ninefold from 2003 to 2006."[4] Similarly, Tom Vanden Brook notes in a *USA Today* article that in 2007 "the U.S. government paid out $315 million in recruiting and retention bonuses. That's a 46 percent increase over 2006. That year, the Reserve paid $216 million in bonuses while falling

5 percent short of its recruiting goal."[5] Given the economics of recruiting, it is hardly surprising that young people heading off to
war engage in a cost-benefit calculus when deciding whether to put
themselves in harm's way. They weigh what they can do if they stay
in the countryside against the military's promises and possibilities,
and they factor in the very real risks that military service today
brings. For an eighteen-year-old soon to graduate from high school
and to become a father, how long would it take to get $20,000 in
cash while taking home $15 an hour working for his uncle's con-
struction company? Then there is the fact that the Army gives its
enlisted members benefits, a pension if they put in the years, and
health care. Every month they serve in combat earns them more
tuition money for a college degree. Sitting there, chatting with the
recruiter in the school office, it all must sound pretty good. In the
age of a volunteer army, the military knows that it must offer something that's better than the status quo.

When the United States embarked on an experiment, under President Nixon, to replace the draft with an all-volunteer force, the
process of finding willing recruits shifted, nearly overnight, from
calling young people to serve out of patriotism or a sense of duty to
creating an image—and offering enticements—that would appeal
to potential recruits. And so it is today that enlistment bonuses
and service-linked tuition remission are part and parcel of young
people's decisions to answer Uncle Sam's call.

Though the recruitment strategies have changed with time,
and the draft hasn't been in place during the lifetimes of today's
recruits, the tradition of young adults from small towns joining
the service endures as a time-honored rite of passage as familiar as
homecoming and the senior prom. In the Ellises of this country, the
military has long been the small-town equivalent of an emergency

exit. The Iowans we call Seekers long to experience the world as much as the college-bound Achievers we met earlier. But since they often lack their college-bound peers' academic and economic assets, breaking free of Liberty County is most easily accomplished via the military. The kids pursued so intently by recruiters like Traylor were the ones *not* cherry-picked and cultivated to be set on a special track. And with rare exceptions, their stepping-stone for leaving the countryside will not be a college degree. For the Seekers, enlisting is just about the only way out.

Therefore, though the calls for national service go out to every corner of the country, the young people most likely to respond are not randomly dotted across the landscape. Neither poor nor rich, the most typical recruits come from families who are middle income rather than middle class. Their parents own homes and live in neighborhoods that are nice but not very nice; they earn their livings as police officers, truck drivers, teachers aides, secretaries, and factory workers, the sorts of jobs in which they wear blue or pink collars but earn enough money to keep up the appearance of a middle-class lifestyle. Neither the best students nor the worst, enlistees are the kids their teachers say never missed an assignment and who were punctual and attentive, the kids whom coaches describe as the solid players who can be counted on to always give 100 percent.[6]

It is no accident that one of the Army's flagship advertisements is set in the Heartland. The spot features a young recruit's father, dressed in the farmer's standard-issue blue jeans, baseball cap, and flannel shirt, and his mother wearing a simple cotton blouse. They appear off in the distance, leaning against a tractor parked on a gravel road beside a harvested field on the family's acreage. Their son, donning the green dress uniform of an Army Ranger, stands at full attention in the foreground. The words "Army Strong" flash onto the screen. The handsome soldier, a model of military discipline, raised in the middle of America, with a cornfield as the backdrop (no doubt a stand-in for amber waves of grain), seems ready to answer his nation's call. Developed in 2006 by McCann Worldgroup, the same firm that sells us on Coca-Cola and Microsoft, the campaign is backed by a $1 billion contract that pays the advertising firm $200 million a year for five years. The people behind the marketing message say they want young people to buy the idea that if they enlist, they "will gain physical and emotional strength, strength of character, and, most importantly, a sense of purpose." The Heartland spot celebrates parents and small-town life and values for producing sons and daughters willing to fight for their country. It is a marketing campaign tailor-made for young people looking to the military as a way out, a message that resonates with the Seekers who want to serve their nation and get as far away from their hometowns as possible. To be sure, this recruitment strategy appears to be working; five years into the wars in Iraq and Afghanistan, the Pentagon reported that "across all three sectors of the Army—the Army, Reserve, and Guard—states in the Midwest and Great Plains have had the smallest drop-off in recruiting." With the war in its sixth year and with more than four thousand American soldiers dead and nearly thirty-one thousand injured, asking young people to put their lives on the line in Iraq and Afghanistan is no easy sell. But in the forgotten, ailing towns of the Heartland, the military offers structure and goals, something between college and the real world—a place where there are barracks instead of dorm rooms, drill instruction instead of classes, and medals and ribbons instead of grades.

Nationally, less than 2 percent of young people between the ages of eighteen and twenty-five are on active military duty, yet a recent report by the Carsey Institute finds that a significantly larger share of the young people fighting and dying in Iraq and Afghanistan come from rural America. For instance, states such as Arkansas, Oklahoma, and Montana send the highest proportion of young people into the military. In contrast, in Connecticut and New Jersey, where sizable numbers of young people attend college, a far smaller number opt to enlist.[7] During the first six months of 2007, 125 troops from ten Midwestern states were killed in Iraq. In June of the same year, Iowa's burden felt even heavier after Private First Class Katie Soenksen became the state's first woman to die in the war and its forty-fifth fallen soldier. After she was killed in an explosion in Iraq, just a few weeks before what would have been the second anniversary of her high school graduation, busloads of people from her hometown of Davenport attended the burial. Somber rituals of this sort have become an all-too-familiar grim reminder to many small towns of the sacrifices made by servicemen and servicewomen—and the effects are felt all the more in a place where everyone watched them grow up.

Even the tiniest schools in the rural counties of the nation's Heartland sponsor Reserve Officer Training Corps (ROTC) programs. In Ellis, eager local recruits seek, and receive, their parents' permission to enlist before their eighteenth birthdays to collect their signing bonuses. That Ellis is a town that sends many of its sons and daughters off to serve is immediately apparent to anyone who visits. The route into Ellis from the west passes a polished granite memorial flanked by life-size bronze statues of soldiers. Carved into the stone are the words "Dedicated to all the men and women who served their country during peacetime and war." The impressive tribute cost the town $30,000. Throughout Ellis, the windows of homes display white banners with blue stars indicating the number of family members on active duty. "Support our troops" magnets festoon the bumpers of every Chevy or Ford truck parked in the Berghoff's Market lot. At the Woodward Thomas VFW on Main Street, mementos, flags, and letters from every local soldier who fought or died in World Wars I and II and Korea sit on permanent display in several long, oak-trimmed glass cases at the front of the hall. Behind the long wooden bar, oversize MIA and POW banners drape the wall alongside the neon Budweiser sign.

Kids growing up in Ellis are baptized into a sort of unselfconscious patriotism that came back in fashion for the rest of the country only after the attacks on 9/11. On Memorial Day and Veterans Day, Ellis's residents stage elaborate celebrations that include the installation (by the local Boy Scout troop) of ten-foot-tall flags along the cemetery path for a quarter of a mile. Marching bands and old men in VFW uniforms honor America and those who fought to protect her. In these moments, home and country become indistinguishable. Veterans of all ages will tell you that they do not trust politicians and fear the government's intrusion into their lives. When they say that they fought for their country, they mean the people back home: their family, friends, and neighbors. They were willing to die to keep Ellis safe and to ensure that the pursuit of happiness—their chance to claim the American dream—would be possible for themselves and the next generation.[8] But despite reverence for the idealized notion of America invoked through flag-waving and veterans tributes, the young Seekers volunteer for reasons that have precious little to do with making sacrifices for the nation.

In the post–Vietnam War era, the idea of serving one's nation became supplanted by the pragmatic understanding that military service exists to support the goals of political leaders making decisions based on grand geopolitical strategic interests.[9] Some Americans might assume that most young people heading off to boot camp are "true believers," that they march into the recruiting center with the words from Toby Keith's anthem for post-9/11 retribution—"Courtesy of the Red, White, and Blue (The Angry American)"—pounding in their ears. When we lived in Ellis, that summer after 9/11, the fever of nationalism ran high all over the country, and rural Iowa was no exception. Drawings by local schoolchildren depicting the collapsing towers and offering tributes to the dead hung on the walls at Ellis's VFW Hall. During the Memorial Day parade, the first prize-winning float, sponsored by a car dealership, featured three young boys depicting one of the most iconic images from the World Trade Center attack, the Iwo Jima–like moment when firefighters flew the American flag over the ruins. All the T-shirts and posters around town called on people "never to forget," and Ellis High School Principal George Herdemann noticed a few more kids than usual flirting with the possibility of enlisting. When an Ellis High alumnus serving with the Army Rangers was photographed for a CNN news segment going on a mission to the mountain region between Pakistan and Afghanistan in search of Osama Bin Laden, everyone tuned in to see the face of their hometown boy flicker on the screen. But even as the terrorist attacks made folks talk about revenge and the need to punish someone, Ellis High's guidance counselor, Dick Grunsky, recalls how serving the country never really overshadowed kids' self-interested motivations for volunteering: enlisting was still, first and foremost, a way out of Liberty County.

Even in places where patriotism isn't riddled with cynicism, the truth is that the reasons young people cite for enlisting are more practical than ideological. All of the service personnel with whom we spoke worried whether their sacrifices would be acknowledged or remembered. None of the soldiers or recruits we interviewed ranked his or her love of country or support for the nation, its policies, or the president as a central reason for enlisting. Most surprising, the young people who volunteered did not see their service as a testament to their support for the war, making a crucial and clear distinction between the unseemly nature of politics and their duty and obligations to the military. Some did not vote and, out of uniform, openly questioned political leaders' motives and beliefs as they pertained to the purpose of the military. It is not that these soldiers were afraid to fight; on the contrary, they accepted the risks with clear courage and practicality but without recklessness or passion. But military service is primarily a means to an end: the best way, probably the only way, "to get some education," "so I can find a halfway decent job" and have a way "to get out of this town" and "see what else is out there." Neither the fact that there is no longer a draft nor the changing nature of conventional warfare in the post-9/11 era alters the underlying reasons for Seekers' choosing this path. In many ways, the Achievers are not all that different from Seekers; it's just that for local kids of modest means who didn't excel academically and weren't encouraged by adults, the military offers a second-best option.

What the Seekers know, with the utmost certainty, is that they do not want to stay in the countryside all of their lives. Interestingly, many of these Iowans choose the Navy; there is something striking about kids raised in the middle of the prairie longing for the sea, as if they seek an experience that is guaranteed to be the polar extreme of the one they knew. The other difference distinguishing the two groups of Leavers—the Seekers and the Achievers—is that the college-bound Achievers are focused on getting a degree and a new life, whereas the Seekers' lives beyond Iowa unfold with precious few signposts guiding them. Seekers possess a powerful, albeit unfocused, longing for something different: there is restlessness and impatience in their wishes, an eagerness for the unknown pushing them to see what the world beyond Ellis might offer. The Seekers are, in a way, romantics.

Marge Germscheid, a military police officer stationed just outside Atlanta, captured that sense when she told her enlistment story. She signed her life away to the Marines after a single conversation, Marge says. "I was like, 'Sure, why not?' I really didn't know why I wanted to join." Marge says the decision, which surprised her entire family, was mostly a gamer's bravado: "I just kind of took a shot. I really didn't know what else was out there, but I knew there was something more than Ellis." For his part, Jason Goetz, a Navy seaman now living in Florida with his wife and three children, could not wait to get as far away from Ellis as possible. The fact that he "didn't have the best grades in the world" and that heading straight to college would not be in the cards led him to view the Navy as "the best thing," if only because it "saved" him "from getting trapped" in Liberty County. He reasoned that volunteering would provide him "some money for school," and, with the Navy's help, he would finish his degree without putting himself or his parents in debt. But with nearly a decade in the service, Jason has just a few courses under his belt and not even a vocational certificate. Though college was always part of his general plan, getting a degree was never as important as "getting out." He reasons, "If I stayed in Ellis, I would have [ended up] marrying the girl down the street or one of my classmates from a grade below or above" and being like "my classmates doing the same jobs they were doing in high school, living in the same place—they haven't done anything." Jason says, "I'll come home and go to Sally's to have a beer, and then it's the same people there, every year, in the same spot. It's like time freezes. And when I come home, it is exactly the same." The thought that he could have basically defaulted into the same life is one that haunts Jason, and his visits home remind him of what he has gained by leaving.

In today's rural economy, in which global market shifts and shrinking wages and benefits threaten daily to betray blue-collar workers, the Seekers manufacture new possibilities for themselves by taking a chance on what the military might provide. William Hansen, a former Air Force mechanic who did a single tour before coming home to Ellis, never took advantage of the military to go back to school and earn a degree. Nor did he put in enough time in the service to qualify for a full pension. Nevertheless, he insists that the time away gave him a space in his life to mature. "I don't know how things would have fallen into place" or even "if they would have," explains William. If he had remained in Ellis, he would have taken the first job he could find out of school and "settled" into what was easy and close. He would be doing "some manual labor and that type of thing," getting no benefits, and taking home the lowest pay in a lousy economy. Although he still ended up in a labor and construction job, it is a stable, full-time job with benefits. He earns enough to cover his expenses and to afford a decent new truck every few years. William reasons that he is doing fairly well—not great, but at least several rungs up from some of the worst jobs in Iowa's economy, largely held by the immigrants toiling at meat-processing plants or on massive factory farms, working for little more than minimum wage on a line where people get maimed and mutilated with disturbing regularity.[10] Such distinctions are subtle to outsiders unfamiliar with the realities of factory work in America's postindustrial new economy, but here in Ellis, the difference between $8 and $15 per hour means living in a house versus a trailer and being viewed as working-class instead of white trash.

Then, of course, military life promises glory and excitement, and for Terry Stead, that was motivation enough. By the time Terry got to high school, he had decided he was headed to the Army. Like Jason Goetz, he lacked the grades for college, and staying in Ellis was at odds with his personality: "If I have a routine, I get edgy and bored. Routines don't work for me." So he told the recruiter, "I wanted the craziest job in the Army, as far as combat goes," and the recruiter obliged by sending Terry to Army Recon, a posting he has had for nearly five years. As depicted in Evan Wright's best-seller *Generation Kill*,[11] recon units operate in small teams and set up observation posts "to see what the hell is going on" in a battle situation. They are the point of the spear in an invasion. Right after completing basic training, Terry was deployed to Bosnia on a mission to "find and secure war criminals," before operatives known to him and his men as "some CIA group" would "come and arrest them." At the time we spoke, back in 2002, less than a year after the terrorist attacks in New York and at the Pentagon, his assignment was training reconnaissance teams for Iraq. Terry said he was putting in "110 percent" at work, and his time in Bosnia had taught him what his guys would need once they were on the ground.

Terry's dedication to the service, training recruits for one of the Army's most dangerous assignments, stands in stark contrast to his high school experience. During those four years, "I never took home a book." Terry does not blame anyone for his disappointing performance back in high school. It is the classic underachiever's tale, he says: "I never even tried." The more Terry drifted off course in school, the more trouble he got into when the last bell of the day rang. Several arrests for possession of alcohol culminated in a more serious DWI charge. A couple of teachers and relatives "didn't want to see me get into more trouble," Terry remembers, but there was no one paying enough attention to "grab ahold of me" and turn the wild, self-destructive teenager in a different direction. It did not help that the Stead family had an established reputation for being from the wrong side of the tracks. They were the kind of people who were frequent flyers in the Ellis jail and had proved, through the conduct of multiple generations of Steads, that they would never amount to enough to get out of Liberty County. Under the rules of small-town life, Terry felt he was written off because of the sins of his people. But Terry admits that his own conduct had done nothing to dispel those judgments. More than anything, what saved him was timing. As things seemed to be veering out of control for Terry, particularly with the law, he collected his diploma and enlisted. As a child, Terry had always admired men in the Army, and it clearly offered the very things he needed most: structure, purpose, clear expectations, and a world where no (negative) expectations were attached to his last name.

Beau Yeost thought entering the military would give him a professional sort of polish, and a recruiter from the Marines eventually coaxed him to sign up. Beau's father had proudly served his country in Korea, and he told all of his sons that the military would challenge them like nothing else. Still, when Beau joined the service, patriotism and honor were lower on his list of priorities than were his own professional development and his hunger to see the world beyond Ellis.

Growing up in Ellis during the farm crisis, the Yeost family lost nearly everything; the banks seized their combines, tractors, and eventually their land, and Beau's father spent a year out of work. Ultimately, the family filed for bankruptcy, and though his parents never split up, their violent fights made Beau and his brothers wonder if divorce would not be a sweet relief. Beau's two older brothers reacted to the strain in part by leaving high school in tenth grade. They bounced between construction jobs and always seemed to be teetering on the verge of an unrecoverable downward spiral; they never landed in prison, but the drinking and partying made it difficult to pay the bills and settle into a family or work routine. Beau traces his brothers' struggles back to listlessness, and their frustration to an aching sense of not knowing how to help themselves: "they just weren't satisfied."

Though Beau managed to get through school and excelled on the baseball team, his grades did not rate him college material. Two years after graduating from high school, he sensed the same creeping disappointment that had overtaken his brothers. Tired of scrambling for seasonal construction jobs around Liberty County, Beau longed for something else. "I needed more," he recalls. "I was twenty. I needed to be on a good path, a better path . . . something more controlled. So I figured I could either go to college or go to enlist." Beau was honorably discharged from the Marines last year, and he is now in Virginia training to be a U.S. marshal. The chance he took paid off, and it pains him to see how so many of the boys he grew up with—his brothers included—still seem so stuck.

Cara Holmeyer hails from a military family: her brother and father served in the Navy, and her mother's father was a decorated World War II veteran. At seventeen, Cara took the early-enlistment incentives for service in the Navy. Senior year, as her friends received thick envelopes from Iowa State and the University of Iowa, she was preparing for basic training. Terrified by student-loan debt, Cara, an above-average student, enlisted because she believed the Navy's promises about allowing her to travel and paying her tuition. Cara reasoned that a life serving her country would bring more satisfaction than would following her friends to community college—the only program she could afford if she stayed in Iowa.

When we first met Cara, back in 2002, she had been out of high school for five years. With half a decade served as a nurse in the Navy, she was weighing her options, trying to figure out if she would reenlist. We spoke less than a year after 9/11, in the months just before war was declared in Iraq. In the national media, talk show hosts and news show pundits debated endlessly, but the word on Cara's base was that a war in the Persian Gulf was inevitable. Cara understood that, given her medical skills, if she signed up again, she would probably be deployed with a Marine combat hospital. When we inquired about what might push her to reenlist, it was amusing—and more than a little surprising—that Cara didn't want to relinquish her medical, specifically orthodontic, care. Showing off her mouthful of braces, Cara explained that her dental work, which she was told would cost more than $30,000 and would never be covered by a regular plan because it was largely cosmetic, was one of the biggest motivations to sign up for another tour and face the dangers of Iraq or Afghanistan.

We weren't surprised to hear later that Cara did choose the perks and spent nine months in a Green Zone hospital in Baghdad, the same hospital featured in the HBO documentary *Baghdad ER* and the place where a nurse was killed when a stray missile struck her as she walked to the gym. It was almost unfathomable that so much of Cara's decision to serve her nation in a time of war came down to something as pedestrian as cosmetic dentistry, but we found young people choosing this path for a range of ordinary reasons: they want a job, an education, health care, to travel, and, in Cara's case, straight teeth.

We caught up with Cara on a visit home to see her parents about a year after her tour. After all her years in the Navy, Cara jokes, she still has never served on a ship or been to sea, except on a cruise with her friends. She is now stationed in Illinois and trains nurses at the Great Lakes Naval Training Center. Her beautiful smile, liberated from the braces, has been paid for by the nation's taxpayers. We ask her the same question we asked during our last meeting: how has serving her country served her goals and plans since she was seventeen? Cara still resists making any judgments about whether her life is better or worse because of the Navy; all she knows for certain is that it has been different. Had she never volunteered, she might have earned a community college degree and be in college by now, but she probably could not have afforded trips to Hawaii or Tokyo. If she had managed to complete her nursing degree and earn her RN, she could be taking home an annual salary of $50,000 or more by now. Then again, without the Navy, she would not have the million-dollar smile. Based on the lives of friends who stayed at home, the odds are good that she would be married and have children. Now, when Cara, who has never married, visits Ellis, she longs to tell her friends, "Go somewhere, see something, move away from home."

Cara approaches disappointment only when she realizes that her military service has not moved her any closer to the reason she enlisted in the first place: a college degree. She is frustrated for herself—and for the new recruits she trains at Great Lakes, who, by not reading the fine print, fall into the same trap. The military assigns recruits to jobs on the basis of test scores, and the realities of life on a base or ship mean there is precious little time to take classes.[12] A bigger problem, she only now recognizes, is that the military's much touted "training" does not translate very well into meaningful job experience in the real world. Cara's military service in Baghdad and her work in naval hospitals as a medical technician mean she has the same duties and responsibilities as a registered nurse with a proper college degree. Yet if Cara left the military tomorrow and tried to find a job at any civilian hospital, it could not hire her. On paper, she is just a high school graduate. Under the specific guidelines for Iowa's hospitals, technically Cara would need to take a six-week certificate course simply to get an entry-level nurse's aide job.

In the end, the biggest difference between today's Seekers and their fathers, grandfathers, and uncles is that while the older generation was drafted, and the GI Bill made it possible for them to attend college, now the kids most ready for college opt out of military service, and those enlisting hope college will somehow happen along the way. It might be tempting to interpret the all-volunteer force and the broadening horizons of higher education as proof that young people are free to take advantage of an expanding list of alternatives. Unfortunately, stories like Cara's make one wonder whether the choices our recruits are making are manipulated by a multimillion-dollar marketing campaign and bare-knuckled recruiters' sales pitches that border on bait and switch. If Cara or her parents could have paid for college—in other words, if she had more options—she would never have enlisted. Although the Navy has provided her with benefits, the benefit with the greatest potential to transform her life, a college degree, still eludes her.

Being a Seeker in a time of war, especially an unpopular one, brings to mind inevitable comparisons to the Vietnam War period. Yet what is so amazing about the Iraq War is how even the most avid antiwar protestors chant, "Support our troops, bring them home." The public may be disenchanted with the decisions of its national leaders, but not with its servicemen and servicewomen. Everyone, no matter what their view of the war, clamors to pay tribute to those in the armed forces with parades, banners, T-shirts, letters and gift packages from the local school, and all the thousands of public displays of pride. When Cara returned home after her year in Baghdad, her entire family flew to California to greet her. On Veterans Day the next fall, Cara became the first woman in Ellis's history to give the keynote speech at the annual parade. Hundreds of people attended; in those first months after coming home, an outpouring of pride and gratitude washed over her.

Whenever people in Ellis see young veterans like Cara, they rush to say how much their sacrifice is valued and respected, and any misgivings about the war are usually kept private in an effort not to disrespect the choices the servicemen and servicewomen made. As in Ellis, there is a silence in America about what the war accomplishes and why these young men and women are enlisting in the first place. Perhaps this is one reason the nation's reaction to the Iraq War seems sedate compared to the turbulence of the Vietnam years. As Ellis's mayor, Lee Ulrich, explains, "Since our young people fight *without a draft*, it gets us out of debating the rightness or wrongness of things." Everyone agrees we should support the troops who fight and mourn those who die, but because they volunteer, Lee says, we get a pass on "asking tough questions about why they are fighting [and what that] means." Under these circumstances, any question about why the troops are there is met with accusations such as "You dishonor our soldiers" and "You don't respect their choices."

Back when a draft compelled young people to serve, Americans rose up in resistance. Now that the military markets itself as a cross between an employment service and a scholarship program, our country gets out of debating how a very particular group of young people is fighting and dying for the nation. It's easy to rationalize that they volunteered to be there, and it's true that today's recruits seek out the armed forces to obtain all the things the marketing campaigns promise: work and steady pay, a place to sleep, training, structure and discipline, education, a chance to prove themselves— and a way out. Previous generations entered the military to answer their nation's call *and* to avail themselves of the opportunities the military offers, whereas this generation is there primarily for the opportunities or, more accurately, because of a shortage of them back home.

When we asked Seekers their opinions about their leaders, particularly President Bush, they sounded just as disaffected and disillusioned about politics and politicians as their peers who never served. Apparently, even those young people who risk their lives on the nation's behalf expect their leaders to disappoint them. Most crucial of all, young people in the military were careful to make a distinction between the government, which is filled with hapless bureaucrats and shameless self-promoters, and their country, which they love. According to Terry Stead, the Army Reconnaissance soldier who served in Bosnia, "Now, I probably shouldn't say this, but the way I feel about our government is that it is very, very crooked, and I think we are just as crooked as any of those governments we are fighting now." All the enlisted military personnel with whom we spoke complained that they felt underpaid and underresourced. And yet, their frustrations and concerns about the politics of war were surgically removed from their support for their comrades and their efforts on the ground. For those who served, their greatest fear, alongside getting hurt or killed, would be that their efforts and sacrifices could and would make no difference.

Perhaps this lack of connection to the deeper sense of patriotism and the national interest is attributable to changing perceptions of military service in the wake of the Vietnam War, when the moral ambiguities were brought home forcefully for even the most hawkish Americans. Seekers have always been realistic about why they are fighting abroad in the first place and perhaps now realize that they no longer need to drape their reasons for enlisting in nationalism. Those of us paying attention may be troubled by the constrained nature of the young enlistees' choices, and how misinformation or misunderstandings in the recruiting process lead a distinct category of young people to serve, while the most privileged are shielded from even meeting recruiters.[13] During the Vietnam War, it was certainly true that draftees in college or with political connections evaded national service, but at least a few could be expected to serve. Some kids—like Beau Yeost and Terry Stead—will take full advantage of what the military can offer, and others, like Cara Holmeyer, will capitalize on the benefits. Still, the reasons that these rural young people enlist reveal much about their lack of options, and as a country, we must be committed to an ongoing dialogue about how much serving our nation actually serves our young people.

FOUR

The Returners

Some people, upon learning how we've lived our lives, are
unable to conceal their chagrin on our behalf, that our lives
should be so limited, as if experience so geographically
circumscribed could be neither rich nor satisfying.
—*Richard Russo*, The Bridge of Sighs

E. B. WHITE FAMOUSLY WRITES THAT there are three types
of New Yorkers: the natives who take their hometown for
granted, the commuters who scurry past the city's greatness to go
from point A to point B, and the transplants who relish every feature of New York life precisely because they have chosen this place
and it is so different from where they started out. In much the same
way, we might say there are three sorts of Iowans, though unlike
New Yorkers, precious few Iowans come to the state from a far-
flung location. And as we have already determined, most Iowans
are Stayers who never venture from their hometowns or outside of
Iowa except for the occasional tourist excursion.

There is a category of Iowans we call Returners, and most of
them fall into the Boomerang category. Boomerangs start out as
Seekers, hungry to experience life someplace else, but with time,
they "boomerang" home after their new lives fail to take hold. Some
drop out of college or leave the military after a three-year tour of

duty. Some just seem deflated after the reality fails to live up to their private wishes. Boomerangs are absorbed back into the Stayer population without anyone paying much attention. However, there are subtle differences. Boomerangs, most of whom complete two-year programs at vocational schools and community colleges, possess more education than Stayers but far less than the Achievers. Back in high school, their class rank put them above the Stayers, "who were down below the low kids," and below the Achievers, whose members always included the top 10 percent of the class. Boomerangs tend to be female, whereas Stayers are overwhelmingly male. Indeed, many Boomerangs say their time in the big city was the two-year equivalent of a bachelorette party, one last fling before their real lives began. At the same time, it's hard to see how they ever gave this new experience much of a chance; on Thursday nights, they pack their bags and drive back to Ellis for the weekend, slipping back into the lives they "put on pause" when they graduated from high school. Then, after a respectable period of time has passed—since teenagers getting married is now seen as archaic and foolhardy—they triumphantly return to Ellis and their waiting fiancés, usually the male Stayers they've dated since high school. Many Boomerangs celebrate weddings in the Ellis Lutheran Church, with receptions at the VFW Hall or one of the nicer hotels in one of Liberty County's bigger towns, the summer after they earn an associate's degree, around the time they turn twenty-one.

Then, there is the rarest sort of Returners: the High-Flyers, who at first glance seem identical to the Achievers because they have prepared to get out of Dodge since grammar school. High-Flyers are the credentialed and upwardly mobile would-be expatriates who set aside their chance at the essentially American wish for self-reinvention when they return home in search of stability. To those unfamiliar with their reasons, it seems as if the High-Flyers abandon the more lucrative and, assuredly, more stimulating possibility of life in the big city to spend their days in the place that time forgot.

Indeed, if we can agree that New York is made up, nearly exclusively, of strangers, newcomers, and individuals unified by an unmistakable agitation, Iowa is the opposite sort of place: a world populated by insiders impatient with those who do not take the deepest sort of pleasure in knowing, with absolute certainty, their place in the world and in abiding by the rules that govern it. If White's most enthusiastic New Yorkers are the transplants, set apart for their restlessness, our Iowans who return have consciously chosen to define themselves by living in a place famous for its seamless continuity.

Bringing Iowa's sons and daughters, prodigal or otherwise, back to small towns is the most popular strategy for reinvigorating those towns. It was the central thrust of former Iowa governor Tom Vilsack's "Come Back to Iowa, Please" campaign, which saw him undertake a walking tour of the state in August 2006 to promote the idea. But the people they want to return in large numbers are High-Flyers, who are also the target of campaigns to retain college graduates in other states as far apart as Maine and Louisiana. The Boomerangs are largely overlooked in these initiatives and are certainly not courted as assiduously as High-Flyers.

The brain drain from rural America, which has helped fuel the urban renaissances of Chicago and the Twin Cities, has left in its wake a cluster of depopulating small towns, where, as one state official quipped, the "seventy-year-olds [are] driving around the ninety-year-olds." The demographers in states losing rural inhabitants tend to describe the phenomenon the way a geologist might explain the depletion of an energy source: with the population shifts of so many young people leaving the prairie, an unstoppable downward cycle is readily apparent through declining school enrollments, sudden spikes in the median age, and rising levels of poverty and social isolation. Given the current and worsening shortages of young people in the countryside, new population infusions will be necessary to sustain community institutions and infrastructure. Growth will come either through attracting new natives from outside the state or through what many consider a far less palatable alternative: immigration. Though a few small towns have famously resisted an influx of immigrants, such as Manassas, Virginia,[1] and Carpentersville, Illinois,[2] others have realized that the single best hope for their communities will be the fastest growing segment of the population in the United States: Latinos. Small towns need to attract people, and, in many instances, they have little control over who those people are. The idea that towns could be transformed rapidly by outsiders with little knowledge of local mores makes people understandably fearful.

The nightmare scenario, troubling more than a few politicians in the Heartland and other states such as Louisiana, Maine, and West Virginia, is how the mass exodus of young people, especially educated ones, threatens not only economic sustainability but also a region's long-term civic viability. A recent study found that nonmetropolitan small towns that had vibrant local capitalism, socially involved churches, and plentiful so-called third places—the stores, cafés, and barber shops that provide a basis for informal life—fared better on several benchmarks of civic welfare.[3] Specifically, the small towns that had a healthy local economy and where people were civically engaged had higher income, less poverty, lower unemployment, and were more likely to retain residents than towns that fared less well on these factors. For towns that lose many of the citizens most likely to take an active role in these aspects of local life, it is hardly a surprise when the common weal declines.

Among policy makers schooled in Milton Friedman's zealous devotion to the power of markets and rational choice, remedying rural out-migration starts with creating the right sorts of incentives to entice constituents to change their behavior. After all, tax refunds can spur consumer spending and the professional military relies on paid volunteers. Governors and senators from Maine to Montana started asking themselves, "What could we offer college-educated twenty-somethings to keep or get them back home?" The answer, they came to believe, was the right bundle of goodies, and, not surprisingly, their first idea was to offer educated young adults tax cuts and credits.

North Dakota and Iowa flirted with plans to exempt residents younger than age thirty from state income taxes. Maine became the first state to offer college students a hefty tax credit to help pay their educational loans if they took jobs in the state after graduation. In 2003, six Heartland senators proposed the most ambitious and sweeping response to rural depopulation to date. One hundred and forty years after the first waves of settlers made their way across the nation's midsection, "The New Homestead Act" would target the more than seven hundred counties nationally that had lost more than 10 percent of their population since 1980. New homesteaders, with credentials in business, medicine, and technology, would look nothing like their nineteenth-century pioneer predecessors. With the offers of venture capital and student-loan forgiveness, state government leaders were strategic and single-minded about the specific sorts of young people they wanted to retain or, in some cases, tempt back.

Governor Vilsack embarked on an even more aggressive effort to recruit educated expatriate Iowans in his "Come Back to Iowa, Please" campaign. State officials mailed more than two hundred thousand letters to out-of-state alumni asking them to return to the state to build their careers and lives. These initial letters were followed up by invitations to attend lavish cocktail parties, where graduates of the state's public universities now living in Washington, D.C., New York City, and Los Angeles would meet the governor. Then, over glasses of merlot and hors d'oeuvres, he would sell them on the idea of bucking the tide and moving back. His pitch would include "C'mon home—times have changed!" and that Iowa was more than just "hogs, acres of corn, and old people." This polished presentation featured salesmanlike flourishes such as "commutes that can be measured in minutes instead of hours" and other sound bites. Yet only one thousand Iowans answered the call as part of Vilsack's "brain-gain" campaign, which fell far short of the governor's goal to attract three hundred thousand new Iowans in the next decade.[4] Still, the campaign itself had set a precedent. The Heartland was losing more than its share of young people, and everyone finally agreed it was time to start fighting to get them back.

In 2007, Vilsack's successor, Governor Chet Culver, expanded

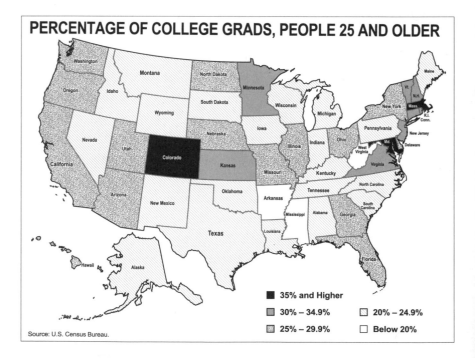

PERCENTAGE OF COLLEGE GRADS, PEOPLE 25 AND OLDER

■ 35% and Higher

■ 30% – 34.9%   ☐ 20% – 24.9%

▨ 25% – 29.9%   ☐ Below 20%

Source: U.S. Census Bureau.

the brain-gain campaign to bait back the Achievers. When the Iowa legislature created the Generation Iowa Commission (GIC) to tap eighteen- to thirty-five-year-olds for ideas on how to keep them in the state, there were more than 250 applicants for the commission's fifteen openings. Building on Vilsack's recruitment initiatives, the GIC also worked on retention—preventing more college graduates from leaving in the first place. A new Web site, hosted by the GIC, features employment opportunities and bloggers who discuss everything from the newest bands to existential debates about their future in Iowa. The GIC originally did not have an appropriation of its own, and the Iowa Department of Economic Development funded its activities, but in 2008 the state of Iowa earmarked $50,000 for the commission's administrative costs.

Kyle Carlson, a twenty-eight-year-old attorney raised in Colfax, Iowa, who earned his BA from Augustana College in Illinois before completing his law degree at Des Moines' Drake University, was tapped to lead the GIC. The first vice chair and current chair of the GIC, Rachel Judisch, is a twenty-nine-year-old speech language pathologist who works in Storm Lake. Other members of the group include Vice Chair Christian Fong, a thirty-one-year-old real-estate market advisor based in Cedar Rapids, and twenty-seven-year-old Emilia Martin, a music therapist from Davenport. From the outset, Carlson understood the uphill battle they faced and that the first phase of work would be to understand why so many promising Iowans were leaving. To do this, the GIC hosted town hall–style meetings all over the state with alumni and recent college graduates. These open forums typically attracted anywhere from fifteen to forty participants, with the largest meeting taking place at the University of Iowa in Iowa City. The GIC also surveyed more than twelve hundred people, nine hundred of whom are defined as "Next Generation," meaning people between the ages of eighteen and thirty-five. They asked respondents about their at-

titudes toward living and working in Iowa. The GIC collated the
findings from the survey along with data that outlined the extent
of the Iowa brain drain and suggested several solutions for plugging
the brain drain.[5]

In the events that the GIC hosted, among the biggest issues
raised was something sounding like adolescent ennui: a shared
sense among young people that there's nothing to do in Iowa. Certainly, if one measures having "something to do" in terms of places
to shop, Iowa might be declared a national disaster area: the nearest
Macy's, Nordstrom's, or Bloomingdale's department stores are in
Minnesota. The entire state, at least in 2008, had just one Apple
Store and a single Ann Taylor, and the ubiquitous Coach purses
and Abercrombie and Fitch apparel that many twenty-somethings
insist on having can be purchased at only three locations in the
state. More difficult to imagine for a college-educated consumer
with money to spend and a healthy caffeine addiction is how 2.9
million Iowans survive with just twenty Starbucks locations. Com-
missioners also were told that, except for restaurant chains and bars
that cater mostly to working men and sports fans, there isn't much
nightlife outside of the small but vibrant arts communities in campus towns.

At the meetings, everyone agreed that the state was severely
challenged in terms of recreational, cultural, and consumer amenities, and much of the brainstorming around solutions centered on
the provision of amenities desired by most college-educated young
adults. In addition, as more people around Des Moines and the Cedar Rapids corridor studied Richard Florida's analysis of the creative
class, local leaders started to believe that this approach offered a solution. Florida himself advised policy makers and addressed crowds
at public forums, and soon there was a great deal of chatter around
the state about encouraging Des Moines to invest in the amenities and services that Florida and his disciples argued would attract

young college grads. There were calls to fund tourism and recreation, and to support an assortment of projects including bike
trails, film and art festivals, and parks. As Kyle Carlson explains,
apologizing in advance for the clichéd *Field of Dreams* reference, to
many people it seemed like the cure for the brain drain had become
"If you build it, they will come." But Carlson was not persuaded
by this analysis or the solution inherent in this logic. To his way of
thinking, there's a big difference between creating a tourist attraction, such as a water park, where someone might spend $100 for
a single weekend outing, and a bike path, which people might use
several days a week. Nor did he think that building "luxury condos"
would solve the region's problems over the long haul. Stemming the
youth-exodus tide would necessitate "giving people an economic
reason to stay, offering them a good career. Then," Carlson said,
"the restaurants and clubs and all the rest will follow."

For Carlson, starting with amenities meant ignoring the more
fundamental issue of adequate job opportunities. There were complaints about the below-average wage levels in the state. Iowa's up-
and-coming young professionals wanted to know, "Why would I
live in Iowa when I can make a lot more money doing the same
kind of job somewhere else?" They had a point. Rural workers make
three-quarters of what workers do in metropolitan settings, and
with student loans to repay and a consumption-oriented lifestyle,
the wage gap, without question, was driving many away.[6] What
troubles Carlson most of all is that many of the jobs available in
Iowa don't require college-educated people. "The statistic that gets
me," he explained, "is that just about 12 percent of the jobs in this
state require a college degree" and this matches up poorly with the
Iowa population: 24 percent of the state's workforce ages twenty-
five to sixty-four has a degree, the proportion being higher for
younger people. Carlson continued, "So any way you cut it, over
20 percent of next generation Iowans are having to decide between

being underemployed or leaving the state in search of an appropriate job. . . . For a long time, the thinking has been [that] all jobs are equal. The state will offer a sweetheart deal to an insurance company to open a call center, which might bring in one hundred jobs at $8 per hour, or even a factory. The thing is, we need to bring in firms like Google, which is setting up operations here. The long-standing strategy of throwing money at any firm just doesn't make sense any longer."[7]

The Google decision, announced in July 2007, to build two data centers near Council Bluffs at an estimated cost of $600 million has been widely hailed as a wise investment because of the availability of cheap land and plentiful electricity, proximity to large numbers of college-educated people, and relative insulation from natural disasters.[8] Just over a year later, Microsoft announced that it would build a data farm at a cost of $500 million in West Des Moines. One reason that these digital titans are setting up shop in Iowa is because of the favorable tax laws that exempt any business from "paying sales tax on the equipment used to build and operate their facilities or on the electricity that powers them."[9] Though neither company's cloud computing center has yet opened, there is an expectation that at least two hundred people will be hired by Google at salaries of at least $50,000, considerably above the median income in the state. Such opportunities are what Carlson and others on the GIC believe will make a difference in the state.

The proposed data centers provide an ironic contrast to the state's technology infrastructure, which the authors of the 2007 Generation Iowa Report described as "a nightmare." For instance, they wrote that if people were to drive "less than 30 miles south of Des Moines and only slightly to the west of Indianola, [they would be in] one of several pockets where high-speed Internet access is only a dream." In Chicago, Minneapolis/St. Paul, or Kansas City, the report's authors lamented, "How long would you have to drive before you found a place without the ability to acquire high-speed Internet access?"[10] So-called wireless and broadband dead zones and technology bald spots were only the tip of the iceberg.

Marketing Iowa has become a big part of the brain-gain plan, and Kyle Carlson recalls the discussions about developing a campaign wherein famous Iowans would sell the state. "[Governor Culver] suggested a marketing campaign with someone like Ashton Kutcher," the Hollywood actor and producer who is originally from Homestead, Iowa. Kutcher grew up on a farm and attended the University of Iowa in the 1990s, where he was a biochemistry major. While working his way through college as a cereal-dust sweeper at the General Mills plant in Cedar Rapids, he won a modeling contest and moved to New York City to work as a professional model. From there he moved to Los Angeles, where he landed a breakthrough part on the sitcom *That 70s Show*. In many ways, Kutcher, though a great success story, is the very embodiment of the problem for Carlson. "He left Iowa and became famous. Focusing on him is really like spreading the message that 'if you leave Iowa, you can go make a name for yourself.'" Instead, the GIC wants to "emphasize people who built their career from the ground up in Iowa."

With the 2008 Olympics, Iowans were excited about the attention that gymnast Shawn Johnson would generate as a favorite daughter, and the state declared October 17, 2007, Shawn Johnson Day. Johnson would be an apt choice to tout the benefits of staying in the state. She has trained all of her career at Liang Chow's gym in West Des Moines, and her success at the 2007 World Championships and the gold and silver medals she won at the Beijing Olympics have catapulted her to stardom and to lucrative endorsement deals. But despite the rigors of Covergirl photo shoots and the post-Olympics gymnastics tour, Shawn is back at her Des Moines high school for her junior year, and she has been an active fundraiser (ironically, with Ashton Kutcher) for flood-relief charities such as the Cedar Rapids Small Business Recovery Fund and the Community Foundation of Johnson County. The fact that Shawn Johnson has eschewed opportunities to train outside the state and has returned to Iowa to finish her high school education could be the basis for an "It's Better in Iowa" campaign, but there is already a series of print and audio advertisements that feature people who have decided to come back to the state.

THE SELLING OF IOWA

The "IOWA *life|*Changing" campaign, sponsored by the Iowa Department of Economic Development, has numerous print, radio, and television spots in circulation that collectively advertise the state as a great place to live and work, especially for the skilled and educated. Several of these ads have done precisely what Carlson suggested. For instance, one of the print ads features a soft-focused, black-and-white photo of Lucas Haldeman with his wife and infant son beside him on a lawn. Haldeman, we are told, is a software engineer who works for a national real-estate dot-com, and he "has recently moved from Southern California, [and] enjoys the good life in Iowa." Off to the side of the picture is one of the GIC's favorite facts: "Iowa is the 8th safest state in America." Underneath, the caption reads, "He's an expert on where to live. And he chooses Iowa." The reader is told that Lucas and his wife, Sarah, grew up in Iowa and left after college to pursue careers in California. But now they're back, and the ad flaunts the contrast between the spacious acreage they own outside Cedar Rapids and the cramped fourteen hundred square feet they rented in the Bay Area. Lucas then exclaims that his mortgage now is less than the rent he paid in California, and the reader should trust his relocation as a sound decision. After all, he "should know [since] he has made a career out of helping people find somewhere to live." Lucas and his wife are the High-Flyers so prized by the state, but all we are told about their return is that "their responsibilities as parents brought them back." It is telling that the ad does not tout work opportunities as much as family benefits.

Another advertisement from 2007 features a young father playing with his daughter, with the caption "They left the Rockies for a higher standard of living." This time, the factoid that Iowa has "the 8th lowest cost of housing" adorns the ad. In the text, we are told that Micah Moore, a Colorado native, moved to Iowa because it is "a great place to raise kids." Micah knew about the quality of life in Iowa presumably because his wife grew up in Harlan, a small town west of Des Moines near the Nebraska border. The Moores were "drawn by Iowa's good schools, lack of congestion and affordable cost of living—particularly its affordable housing." Micah is quoted as saying that they sold their "suburban home in Denver on a very small lot, and for close to the same price, we could buy our dream house on five acres here in Iowa."

The similarities with the first ad are striking: again we see a young white family repeating the mantra that Iowa is an ideal place to raise children. Plus, one can purchase significantly more property in Iowa than in the creative-class boomtowns. Left unsaid, however, are the limited opportunities for work and any sense of the compelling personal reasons that induce many people to return. In the first ad, the couple was originally from Iowa, and, in the second one, Ms. Moore is also from the state. It is not a stretch to guess that personal reasons played a role in both couples' decisions to return, nor is it a surprise that this is not highlighted. Herein lies one of the main challenges for states like Iowa that need to induce Achievers to return. If personal reasons or familial obligations draw people back, then the low-cost housing, good schools, and low crime rate, all of which can be aided by state action, may be irrelevant. The second problem with these campaign ads is that they ignore the needs of young single adults. Such messages do nothing to diminish the negative image of Iowa as a state that, in the words of one young Iowan we spoke with, echoing Vilsack's earlier observation, has "nothing but corn fields, hog farms, and old white people."

Marketing Iowa more effectively and changing it to make it more attractive to the young people who are most likely to leave are not one and the same thing. From the beginning, policy makers in Iowa and other brain-drain states seemed more interested in doing the former, not the latter. Who could blame them? Selling what you are is much easier than changing to become something else. Most revealing of all is how, during the Generation Iowa open forums, people complained about the shortage of singles in the state. There were jokes about how the state should start a dating service if it wanted to keep young people from leaving. In many ways, the IOWA *life*|Changing campaign is actually saying that when you feel like settling down and want more bang for your buck in real estate, then maybe you'll come home. But other advertising campaigns seem to better understand the unique needs of talented twenty-somethings. For instance, the people behind the hugely successful iPod and iPhone campaigns understand that selling young people on a lifestyle requires an innate sense of what your target population wants and needs. Curing recent college graduates of what Nebraska's director of economic development terms "big-city syndrome" is going to take the same kind of approach, tapping into the wishes and aspirations of the target demographic.

At the Generation Iowa Commission community meeting, some young Iowans primed to leave the state complained that Iowa was too traditional and old-fashioned. Bubbling beneath the surface of such statements was the sense, particularly among those attending the state's flagship universities, that Iowa's good schools, fine quality of life, and low cost of living are not appealing enough to overcome its stifling parochialism and intolerance. "Iowa is a homogenous 'white' state" was a familiar refrain, and there was a great deal of discussion at these forums about the state's disappointing record on matters of race and diversity. Though Iowa has no painful legacy of slavery, its small black population would hardly regard the state as a model of racial harmony and integration.

In a state that boasts one of the nation's highest average SAT scores and lowest high school dropout rates, the number of African American students in Iowa completing high school has actually fallen since 1980. This has occurred despite the fact that high school graduation rates were on the rise nationally. It is also startling that in Iowa, where 94 percent of the population is white, there are thirteen African American prisoners for every one white inmate, ranking Iowa among the worst in the nation in terms of incarcerating racial minorities at disproportionate rates.[11] Fundamental racial inequalities play out not only in education and incarceration but also in household income; in 2000, black households had median incomes 36.8 percent less than the state average.

There are other sources of diversity in Iowa, most notably the recent influx of Latinos. Here, too, the recent record on tolerance is inconsistent. For instance, in 2007, there was a setback to efforts to open up Iowa to non-natives when the Court of Appeals upheld laws that had made Iowa the twenty-seventh state to make English the official language and to not print any public notices in other languages. Though mainly symbolic, what message did it send when Governor Vilsack—who had called for the state to attract hundreds of thousands of immigrants to settle in Iowa by 2020 and traveled around the country assuring Iowa's young expatriates that the state had changed for the better—signed the English-only law into effect?

Richard Florida argues that highly mobile, creative people gravitate toward places such as the San Francisco Bay area, where cultural vibrancy and openness are major attractions. Florida famously measures diversity through the number of immigrants ("the melting pot index") as well as the number of rock bands and level of artistic activity, which he dubs "the bohemian index." But Florida also interprets the presence of large gay and lesbian populations as another indicator of a region that attracts entrepreneurial talent. Altogether, the factors are "indicators of a culture that enables entrepreneurs to mobilize." The supporters of the GIC agreed that the three T's—talent, technology, and tolerance—would be critical for transforming the economy, and in their 2007 report they called for the state to encourage and support more racial and ethnic diversity and invest in building a more vibrant cultural scene. But regarding the last part of Florida's indicators, the issue of sexuality, the GIC report made no statement. Sexual diversity and advocacy of gay rights—especially the hot-button issue of same-sex marriage—were not topics that anyone was prepared to take on publicly. Iowa City, home to the University of Iowa, is one of a handful of places throughout the entire Midwest where a registry for gay couples even exists. This allows two adults of the same sex in a relationship of "mutual financial and emotional support" to register as domestic partners. But despite the existence of this registry, in Iowa the laws remain hazy about whether gay couples can adopt children. In a quintessential tension of the "don't ask, don't tell" era of gay rights, single individuals who happen to be gay are permitted to adopt, but the law makes no provision for cross-adoption by a same-sex partner. In addition, Iowa City is anomalous in the state in this and other regards, and what happens there should not be taken to represent the leanings of most Iowans, since for them Iowa City has always been "where all the weirdos are."

Most recently, though, the flashpoint of conflict in Iowa has been gay marriage. In 2007, a Polk County judge lifted the state's ban on gay marriage after declaring its "Defense of Marriage Act"—first passed in 1998—unconstitutional. The next day, a dozen couples appeared at the Polk County Courthouse to apply for marriage licenses. But by lunchtime, the same judge had placed a stay on the decision, and the county recorder declared that no licenses would be granted or honored. Republican House Minority Leader Christopher Rants declared, "I can't believe this is happening in Iowa," and used the incident to call for a harsher and more binding state constitutional amendment banning gay marriage altogether in Iowa.[12] Governor Chet Culver, who had formed the GIC, would later say that although the issue is divisive to Iowans, his opinion is that marriage ought to be between a man and a woman. A case that stems from the initial Polk County ruling reached the Iowa Supreme Court on December 9, 2008, and a University of Iowa poll taken in November 2008 illustrated the divided opinion in the state over the issue. The poll "found that 28.1 percent of those surveyed support same-sex marriage, while another 30.2 percent support civil unions, but not marriage. A third of those questioned oppose any recognition of same-sex couples, with about 10 percent having no opinion or refusing to answer."[13]

In the end, all of the virtues that the state wants to trumpet—quality of life, safety, and low cost of living—seem more likely to score high marks among those young people who settle into the same pattern as their parents' or grandparents' generation—that is, by marrying early, having kids, and entering the full-time labor force soon after high school, often without a college degree.[14] What Iowa wants to sell is not really what many young people want to buy, particularly those who are searching for a mate, are working toward a demanding professional career, or enjoy spending much of their income on music, movies, and merchandise rather than a mortgage. Today's twenty-somethings delay their entry into adulthood because of an economy that demands a longer commitment to education; there is now an extended transition into everything from marriage to career. But what Iowa, and other places like it, can offer these young adults are the very things that become appealing only after one has the trappings of an adult life. Kyle Carlson complains that Iowa is mired in the rut of a dying agro-industrial economy that revolves around a way of life to which his peers have only the most tenuous ties. He fumes at the fact that the state's new minor-league hockey franchise is called The Chops,[15] because "it's just another sign of how we can't let go."

The irony is that while the state's political elite scrambles to write reports and host town hall forums, when you talk to the handful of young people bucking the trends and building lives in Iowa, people like the GIC's own Kyle Carlson, their stories suggest that the economic incentives politicians promote may not be the silver bullet that everyone hopes to find. It is revealing that Carlson, who dedicates much of his time and energy figuring out how to retain more young people in Iowa, says he returned mostly because he got "lucky." Staying close had little to do with a commute "measured in minutes instead of hours" or the low cost of housing. Carlson has built a life in his hometown of Waverly because he placed the personal above the professional. "My whole family is here. I have younger siblings, including a thirteen-year-old brother, who I wanted to be around." It's also relevant that Carlson's chosen profession as a political lobbyist means that "contacts and relationships are more important than anything." Building upon political capital that he started to acquire in law school makes it possible for him to pursue his chosen career. And yet, even with the potent combination of Carlson's professional and private motivations, had he not found his job "just in time," he would have retooled himself to be attractive to employers outside Iowa and followed the exodus of talent out of the state. The often serendipitous journey of a High-Flyer returning to a small town illustrates just how difficult it is to predict who will come back—and why.

• • •

Liz Volker settled in a town near Ellis not because of marketing campaigns or tax cuts but because of other priorities. Liz attended medical school at the University of Iowa, and in 2003 she returned to the countryside and joined a practice that she eventually took over. Her new office is a forty-minute drive from Ellis, and her husband, Bill, works as an administrator at a Cedar Rapids community college. Liz met Bill at Ellis High. Both of them attended the University of Iowa, and they married just a few weeks after their graduation. On track to live the quintessential professional Achiever life, the Volkers decided to come home. Most of their college friends could not understand why they abandoned big-city opportunities for life in a small town. But for Liz and Bill, money didn't compare to other concerns. "Probably the biggest motivating factor" in returning to the Iowa countryside, Liz said, "was my family. I want to be close to my extended family. . . . I chose to stay here because I wanted to raise my children [here]. I enjoy Iowa." Then there was the family-friendly environment; attending college and medical school convinced the couple that they were not "big-city people." "We like the rural areas. I like a smaller school system. I like to think my kids will have smaller classroom sizes, individual attention. We really like the small-community feel, knowing your neighbors, getting involved in the community, knowing your people at church, just feeling a part of the community and being able to contribute to [it]." Though personal issues and preference for a certain quality of life topped their list of priorities, the Volkers understand how this choice works against their economic interests.

Liz concedes that for medical professionals facing huge debt, loan forgiveness may be a powerful incentive that regions can offer. The shortage of doctors and dentists in rural areas has become such a national crisis, in fact, that the nation's largest insurers offer loan-repayment programs for physicians willing to set up shop in underserved areas. And as Liz knows all too well, six out of every ten Iowa counties are underserved.[16] The devastation of the hollowing-out process has severely hampered access to medical care, and the constricting of basic medical services in this rapidly aging region means that more people must drive hours just to see a dentist or doctor who will accept Medicaid. Without medical professionals in many small towns, Liz says, "Main Streets start shrinking," and "the downtown areas are dying." Places like Ellis and nearby Belleview, where Liz practices, struggle to reverse the trend but, as she says, "it's hard to compete."

The other loss inherent to a shortage of doctors and other professionals is a dearth of civic leadership. As a small-town doctor, Liz's profession comes with huge privileges and heavy obligations: "Community involvement is definitely expected. I'm on the board of the nursery school, those sorts of things. You're targeted by different school groups to donate both money and time. I think in those kinds of positions, people look up to you and expect that level of community involvement, and if you don't live up to that, it can hurt your business."

Overall, Liz has no "lasting regrets" over her decision to return to a small town, though she admits to some second-guessing. She concedes that it has been more of a struggle here to run a small country practice than it would have been if she'd become an associate in the established Des Moines medical group that also made her an offer. Although Liz has some bad days, she says that "those feelings don't last very long."

Because most of the people coming back are essentially acting against their own financial interests, Liz does not place much hope in the brain-gain campaigns. Only a select group of kids who could be successes someplace else walks away from big-city life. And the trouble is, when you ask that select few why they came home, their reasons have little to do with anything policy makers can offer. The other problem is that although the state wants more Achievers to return, only a minority ever do: just 40 percent of those graduating from Ellis High remain in Liberty County ten years after finishing high school, and only a handful of these are sought-after and prized professionals such as Liz Volker.

BOOMERANGS AND THE SHORT WAY HOME

When most Returners come back home, they do so precisely because the world beyond Ellis fails to live up to their expectations. Sometimes a stint in the military does not deliver the expected career or degree. Maybe college wasn't the right fit, or they just couldn't settle in and found life in a city to be too big, noisy, and overwhelming. More often than not, it seems coming home is a runner-up prize for what might have been. Despite all the attention focused on tempting more High-Flyers back, the truth is that the people most likely to return in many ways resemble those who never left: the Stayers.

When twenty-nine-year-old William Billings left for college, the plan was to get a degree and find a job as an engineer out of state. After one semester, the temptations of the college party scene, combined with his bottoming-out grades, made him realize that getting a degree wasn't such a good fit. "I did really well my first semester at college [and] was in the threes as far as academics. Then when I turned nineteen . . . I just kinda went downhill [and] ended up dropping half my courses, so that [semester] just went 'bye-bye.' And . . . my third semester . . . I didn't go to class at all, [so] I came home and told my folks that 'college isn't right for me right now.' They said, 'All's we're doing is dishing out money for something, and you're not getting nothing out of it.'" These days, William is back home in Ellis, working as a welder at Safeguard and raising two kids with his wife, Darlene, not far from her folks. William says that the only difference between him and the guys who never set foot on a college campus is the student loans he's paying off.

Thirty-year-old Melissa Dribben was a pre-med student at the University of Iowa before she dropped out. The affluence, pace, scale, and intensity of the university made Melissa, the youngest daughter of Ellis dairy farmers, realize that she wanted no part of the world beyond Liberty County. Although she would go on to finish her degree, she would never make it to medical school. She now works as a bank manager and is happily married to a man from an adjacent county whom she met while waitressing to put herself through school. College was not like high school, and Melissa recounts that "it was very intimidating. . . . It's not like you walked to school and knew everybody on campus." She continues, "I didn't like Iowa City, basically. I didn't like college; it was a whole bunch of what I wasn't used to. I was used to small-town Iowa. . . . And this was little rich kids from Chicago . . . and that just didn't fit my lifestyle. And it was a lot more open-minded than I was used to in terms of ideals and people and clothing and everything. It blew me out of the water. I wasn't prepared for all that."

For Annaretha Davison, who managed to finish a teaching degree after moving back to Ellis and getting engaged to her high school boyfriend, college life was one of the reasons she came home. "Ellis is such a small town. You have such limited opportunities to experience different things. It was just that when I was at Iowa State, it was huge, [and] I was overwhelmed. I was just the little fish in the big pond. I went from being the popular girl in a small town to being this nobody on the floor with sixty girls. It was daunting and intimidating and very frightening to me. In Ellis, people were very giving and generous with . . . praise and encouragement, but it was almost a downfall to me because I was starting to thrive on it. . . . And when you get to college, they don't do that. . . . So academically, I did well, but emotionally, my first year of college was a big struggle for me." This emotional stress led the high school honor student to indulge in such heavy partying that, by her sophomore year, she feared she was on the verge of developing a drinking problem. Things improved when she returned to Ellis and embraced the fact that she was not wired for life beyond her hometown. She says that growing up in Ellis had "made her addicted to the affirmation and attention." At college, she learned she needed the comfort and security of being in a place where people who have known you all your life encourage you to be the person you were meant to be.

To the kids who come home, the values of the world beyond do not match up with what they believe to be important. Twenty-four-year-old Madeline Spencer tried out college for a year, but she moved back home so that she could commute to a nearby "suitcase school" and finish a two-year degree in medical administration. Now married with a young son and working part-time in a small newspaper's advertising department, the world of stylish single women is something she sees only on television. Marriage and family, in comparison, were real, concrete, and possible. To her, giving up a four-year college degree in accounting was something she had to do because that life didn't fit the person she was, largely because of her hometown. "Maybe if I had grown up in a big city, like Minneapolis, [I would have wanted a four-year college degree and a career] . . . [but] I don't want to even try to be a Superwoman," she said. "I'd rather hang out on the floor with my kids."

Claire Miller, a community college graduate—who, as is typical of Returner women, wed her high school boyfriend at a young age—says that the world beyond the countryside just seemed too "overwhelming." Rather than seeing college as an opportunity, she felt that it was an obstacle to be overcome. "I didn't want to leave high school my senior year. I was scared to go anywhere. . . . I knew I could do well in high school, but what was college going to bring?"

The rejection of the sort of life many Returners encountered upon leaving Ellis often involved a fear of the unknown or of dealing with difference. Kay Billings, a single mother working at a nursing home, was quite blunt about her unsettling encounters during a year of community college in Cedar Rapids. "In a small town, I never had to be around anybody [whom I didn't know], anybody of a different color, race, or anything, and when I got [to college] I was petrified. Like the first week I was bawling 'cause I was scared to death." A thirty-year-old nurse named Marsha Allan, who is just finishing her teaching certificate to work with preschoolers, recounts a similar experience being in the dorms at her college in Omaha. "There were [so many] African Americans. . . . My first week I saw a person overdose on drugs, and another week there was a drive-by shooting. . . . They were scary." Though the drive-by shooting occurred a fair distance from the dorms, these events, which typically involved African American victims and offenders, served to reinforce any negative preconceptions Marsha may have had about racial minorities. The events were extreme and aberrant, but for Marsha, they came to epitomize life away from Ellis.[17]

Many Returners are women who have some higher education credentials and bring back certain skills with them. On the face of it, they are different from the mostly male and less-credentialed Stayers. But often their experiences away are negative rather than positive, and so in terms of how they view the world, these Returners share many of the fundamental views of the Stayers, in which experiences of diversity are juxtaposed with the safety and comfort of knowing everyone in a small town, and the disorder and unpredictability of large towns and cities is contrasted with the easy predictability of life in a place where everyone knows your name.

These types of Returners far outnumber the mercurial High-Flyers, and their experiences away are markedly different. High-Flyers generally have a more positive experience away from Ellis, and the decision to return is, for them, also a positive one. High-Flyers share many of the affective ties of the other Returners, but they have a different profile in terms of their educational and professional qualifications. Most important is the fact that they bring with them much-needed skills. At heart, High-Flyers know how important they are to the small towns they return to, and many are aware of the various expectations people have of them. Boomerangs are less conscious about their role in maintaining small towns, not because they don't care, but because of the reasons for their return and because they are not as overtly courted or feted as High-Flyers. It is noteworthy that none of the IOWA *life*|Changing campaign ads featured the story of a young Iowan with a Boomerang profile.

RETURNERS AND THE FUTURE OF SMALL TOWNS

One way to save small-town Iowa will be attracting new people to come settle there. Liz Volker believes that this is the greatest hurdle facing the state. People in small towns must learn to "outstretch their hands to anybody entering the community . . . [to] get them involved and make them feel welcome," she said. Too often, people can get "into their own cliques and sometimes keep to themselves," but it is important to "be open to change." In a world where, as she jokes, "we don't have a lot of multicultural training," embracing diversity is no easy sell. For Liz, the problem is simply that many people in small towns "have never been exposed to people from other cultures and other walks of life, which is the biggest plus of postsecondary education." It is ironic that Liz notes that college offers a kind of multicultural training. One of the greatest challenges facing Iowa is coming to terms—even welcoming—the inevitable changes in the makeup of its population. The fact is that a viable future for many small towns may lie in being open to the very sorts of multicultural experiences that so many Returners flee.

It would be too simplistic to characterize High-Flyers as being

wildly open cosmopolites and Returners as narrow-minded isola-
tionists. Neither designation is completely accurate; both groups
hold complex views about newcomers and integration. Liz notes that
integration is a two-way street, and she is made uneasy by settlements of Orthodox Jews in Postville, who, in her opinion, are coming
to "find a spot that's remote enough that they can create their own
community. I'd love to see those groups come in, integrate in the
communities, still retain the uniqueness of their religion, who they
are, practice as they want but also intermingle with the community."

As we have seen, in many parts of the Heartland, the thinking on
how to stem the brain drain and begin the brain gain has centered
on attracting the best and brightest back. States such as Maine,
Michigan, Iowa, and Louisiana have initiated campaigns to ensure
that college graduates stay close. In Iowa, this strategizing has
evolved to include gubernatorial receptions around the country and
a local commission charged with developing an action plan. Parallel
to these statewide campaigns are nascent grassroots efforts wherein
small towns are getting into the business of promoting themselves
and trying to attract more High-Flyers.

Halfway through the summer we lived in Ellis, we received an
invitation from the local branch of the Rotary to address its weekly
lunch meeting. We had become friendly with several local board
members, and although they were interested in hearing about our
research project, they had a more pressing concern: they needed a
plan to attract more professionals to Ellis. Since we had spoken to
many locals who had become doctors, lawyers, and other professionals with advanced degrees, what advice did we have to make
Ellis more appealing to that desirable set? As we pondered the question, the conundrum posed by the Ellis Rotarians and their civic
and political counterparts elsewhere in the Heartland soon became

apparent: Ellis has the outward trappings of a civically vibrant small town, including a state-of-the-art library and a sumptuous outdoor swimming pool, but even with such amenities, the town had trouble hiring a doctor for the local hospital.

At the time, we didn't have an answer for how a small town can become a honey pot for High-Flyers, though we believed that building amenities certainly couldn't hurt. Since that time, the Iowa brain-gain campaign has gathered speed and has been mirrored in other places with programs such as the Michigan Cool Cities Initiative, created in 2003 to keep college graduates with high-tech degrees in the state. The Cool Cities Initiative was crafted straight from the Richard Florida playbook: endow places with amenities, a jazz bistro or a multipurpose park, and you will attract, or keep, the much sought-after "knowledge workers" who are "leaving the state in alarming numbers." So in the summer of 2003, Michigan governor Jennifer Granholm issued an invitation to the mayors of every major Michigan town and city to institute a local Cool City Advisory Group, and later that year the Cool Cities State Advisory Group met for the first time. The idea behind Cool Cities is straightforward: you "build a cool city and they—young knowledge workers and other creative class members—will come."[18] However, the program's results have been far from encouraging. A recent editorial in the *Detroit News* noted that despite the initiative's best intentions, many college graduates still leave the state to find jobs.[19] The crux of the issue is that building a cool city means very little when there are no jobs, and a recent survey by the Michigan Economic Development Corporation found that 53 percent of approximately thirty thousand "knowledge" graduates in the state university system said they left the state for a better job, while only 4 percent said they left because of the limited opportunities for a social and cultural life.[20] Michigan's embrace of the creative-class analysis has not borne the fruit that many expected.

Other states have crafted their own version of a brain-gain campaign. In Louisiana, where Governor Bobby Jindal in 2006 made retaining graduates from the state universities a priority, State Representative Neil Abramson has proposed helping one hundred college graduates who pledge to live and work in Louisiana for five years get tax rebates up to a maximum of ten thousand dollars to help them buy a house.[21] In West Virginia, Governor Joe Manchin promised loan forgiveness for recipients of a state scholarship if they would work in the state after graduation. And in Maine, the state launched, in January 2008, Opportunity Maine, a program designed to provide debt-relief incentives to students who graduate from Maine colleges and stay in the state to work. In a variation on the theme of debt relief, Opportunity Maine allows individuals who take out college loans or businesses who agree to pay off a student loan to be eligible for tax relief.

One thing that is readily apparent from the Returners we spoke with is that the various campaigns to bring talented people back or encourage them never to leave may be missing the point. Economic incentives and cool cities are all well and good, but High-Flyers may have a more personal reason for returning, and Achievers may have a more fundamental reason for leaving. States and towns that experience a siphoning-off of young people whom they have prepared and educated and, in many cases, funded can't really legislate for people to make what seems an irrational decision to be paid less to work in a small town. Nor can these same bodies easily match new job opportunities that exist in creative-class hubs without a substantial investment in infrastructure and incentives to entice companies.

So what can be done to better match the goals of the brain-gain campaigns with the realities of Returners? First, just as Stayers are underinvested in compared with Achievers, there is an analogous lack of focus on the Boomerangs in favor of the High-Flyers. Most

Returners we spoke with were not professionals, but they do have credentials and skills. Although members of this group are not the usual targets of debt forgiveness and other incentives, future campaigns should take them into consideration, since they represent an often overlooked but nonetheless crucial source of vitality for depopulating small towns. Such investments might also make returning less of the negative event for Boomerangs that it seems to be at the moment. It would be a mistake to underinvest in people who are already situated to help small towns, and so future policy that is crafted to entice Returners should expressly widen its scope to include *all* those who decide to come back, not just the members of the professional class.

Second, as Kyle Carson and others[22] have pointed out, what is most needed to reverse the outward flow of educated graduates is a strong and diversified job market with opportunities for young professionals to pursue their careers locally. This requires investment, infrastructure, and a not insignificant amount of good fortune, but there are examples of how it can be done. The so-called Minnesota bioscience zone, which encompasses areas around Rochester, Minneapolis, and St. Paul, was created in 2004, and it offers a package of tax incentives for bioscience start-ups willing to set up shop in the region.[23] The bioscience zone seeks to build on related local infrastructure, which includes the University of Minnesota, the Mayo Clinic, and industry leaders including 3M and Medtronic. The architects of the program predict robust job growth as more companies relocate there.[24] It is too early to declare whether the bioscience zone has been a success, but it is noteworthy that the counties that encompass the zone have had significant population growth, especially of young people, during the past decade and a half.[25]

Third, one of the most pressing and obvious needs of places that are hollowing out is for qualified professionals, especially in medical fields. What would help here is a coordinated campaign that provides compelling incentives for doctors, dentists, and other medical professionals to practice in underserved areas after graduation. Such programs could start before college with a high school mentoring program in which interested students would essentially shadow medical professionals and get a sense of their jobs. A second component of this program would be a tuition grant for students willing to commit for a five- or ten-year period to an underserved area after graduation. This way, future medical professionals are identified early, and they enter into a commitment to return home in exchange for tuition payment. Small towns would not have to rely solely on High-Flyers making serendipitous decisions to be closer to family, and the long-term benefits to underserved areas will more than repay the costs involved.

The task for small towns that are on the thin edge of the hollowing-out process is a tall one. We suggest that towns encourage the Boomerangs with as much zeal as is accorded the more credentialed High-Flyers because, in many cases, the ability of Boomerangs to strengthen the local economy and contribute actively to civic life is discounted. Such an oversight at such a critical time for many small towns will be costly, and overcoming it will require some fresh thinking. In this, we believe that policy concerning those who return needs to focus on opportunities more than on amenities, at least at the outset. High-Flyers can and should be cultivated before they go to college, and Boomerangs have a great deal to contribute and ought to be included in any future initiatives.

What Can Be Done to Save Small Towns?

ELLIS, 2005

It is a steamy August evening in Ellis, and the air-conditioned coolness of the high school conference room provides a welcome relief from the humidity that drapes itself across the plains this time of year. Two years have passed since we interviewed more than a hundred young people for the Heartland Project, and the purpose of our trip to Ellis High School now is to share some of the findings with the principal and the school board at a specially convened closed meeting. We are anxious about the meeting because we suspect that some of them will find parts of our analysis difficult to accept. One by one, the board members file in, exchanging greetings with the easy familiarity of people who have known each other for a long time. They seem expectant and upbeat, confident that they will receive a glowing report about how Ellis has put the young adults we interviewed on the right track.

Principal George Herdemann is a tall, quiet-spoken, efficient, and intense man who prefers to let others talk while he absorbs information. In his six years in charge, he has led Ellis High with a steady hand through the tricky process of consolidating with the neighboring district of Stearns. He is every inch the modern administrator and knows the value of maintaining test scores and graduation rates. During his tenure at the helm of Ellis High, he has been aided by a school board of like-minded locals who pride themselves on the school's high academic standards and the diverse extracurricular activities.[1] Despite not having enough students to avoid a merger and now having a dreaded hyphen in their school name, Ellis people still look upon Ellis-Stearns High School as theirs and believe that the successful graduates who venture forth reflect well on the community.

For this meeting, we prepared an eighty-five-hundred-word report that we circulated to the board a week in advance. We present demographic information on the nearly three hundred former Ellis High students we surveyed and have in-depth information on more than one hundred young adults, along with countless anecdotes. In the final section of the report, we highlight what these young people said about their time at Ellis High and what has helped or hindered them since. The report also describes the Leavers, Stayers, and Returners, and, during the talk, as we summarize the descriptions of each group, the board members nod in recognition. That each category of young adults has a different perspective on both the experience of attending Ellis High and what should be done differently is also unsurprising to Herdemann and the parents and residents at the meeting. Many Leavers, especially the ones who attended college, would have liked to have been better prepared academically and socially, and many Stayers said that their education should have been focused on providing the concrete skills they would need in their working lives instead of on teaching so-called irrelevant, abstract academics.

The body language around the table, largely nods and smiles of agreement, indicated how these findings were merely confirming what the principal and his board already knew, and so we decided to venture further than the report had gone. We took a provocative line and rhetorically asked, "You do realize, don't you, that because you do your job so well here, that you are basically making sure that the best students leave Ellis, and the odds are they won't come back? And at the same time, you spend very little of your resources on most of those who stay or return." We expected people to bristle, perhaps even becoming defensive about Ellis and the school. But to our astonishment, no one on the board said anything; several people merely shrugged their shoulders and grinned ruefully. Herdemann was the only one to speak. "This is the job we set out to do," he stated matter-of-factly.

The meeting concluded shortly thereafter, and we stayed to talk with Herdemann. We inquired why he wasn't more worried about the idea that Ellis was sowing the seeds of its own decline. Herdemann nodded thoughtfully and replied that most people felt it was their job to ensure that the best kids got all the help they needed, and that, inevitably, meant that they would move away. Certainly, he understood that the school plays a pivotal role in this process, but he concluded that the job of an effective educator was to nurture and send off talented youth, despite the fact that doing so meant the town was slowly committing suicide.

DISCOVERING THE RURAL CRISIS

A cabinet-level appointment, assuredly, does not guarantee an issue receives as much attention as it deserves in American politics, but the existence of such a post offers a crude sort of ranking of the issue's priority in the national agenda. Experts and policy makers in urban affairs would never say that the crisis of the inner city garners the public and political attention it warrants, and yet it is noteworthy that there is a secretary-level member of the cabinet whose job is to advise the president on housing and urban affairs.[2] Rural development, interestingly enough, falls under the Department of Agriculture; indeed, there is an undersecretary of rural development, but the position is fourth in line at the department. In practical terms, what this means is that this undersecretary reports to the undersecretary for marketing and regulatory programs, who reports to the undersecretary of Agriculture for farm and foreign agriculture services, who reports to the deputy secretary of Agriculture, before it gets to the secretary, who talks directly to the president. It is fair to conclude that rural development is not a major concern in national policy.

To be sure, members of the research community (ourselves included) are no less culpable. The urban and community section of the American Sociological Association has one of the organization's largest memberships, and the top graduate programs at Harvard, and the universities of Chicago, Pennsylvania, and Michigan train dozens of researchers for careers in finding solutions for poverty, family breakdown, academic failure, and crime in the urban milieu. Meanwhile, rural sociology survives as a relatively minor subdiscipline pursued by a small and committed band of scholars. Despite the iconic place the Heartland inhabits in the national psyche, rural policy remains the most obscure of concerns.

And so, despite the auspicious start for the research on Middle America, in the form of Robert and Helen Lynd's masterpiece *Middletown,* and the enduring symbolic salience of small-town America in the national imagination, serious inquiries into the challenges of modern rural life have not yet captured the wider public's attention. Major newspapers assign reporters to cover the suburban and urban beats, but the *Washington Post, Wall Street Journal, New York Times,* and even Fox News, the self-styled populist voice of the nation's media, have no equivalent rural-issues correspondents. Pundits such as David Brooks or Bill O'Reilly earn their livelihoods touting the moral superiority and wisdom of small-town values, although one doubts if the University of Chicago–educated Brooks or O'Reilly, who spent his formative years in the quintessential American suburb of Levittown, New York, and earned degrees from Boston and Harvard universities, has ever sat around the kitchen table talking with people who live in a trailer or on a working farm.[3] On the other end of the spectrum, Jon Stewart and Arianna Huffington use small towns and assorted other red-state stereotypes as their own ideological punching bags. Broad caricatures and media constructions of the NASCAR Dad, Joe the Plumber, Hockey and Wal-Mart Moms, Main Street, evangelicals, small-town racists, and gun nuts are about as useful as any stereotype. Even with the incessant shouting in the culture wars, both sides ignore, gloss over, or just plain don't care about the truth of crystal meth or oxycontin epidemics, depopulation, rural poverty, the extintction of the family farm, deindustrialization, immigration, crime, job loss, economic decline, and environmental threats created by contaminated groundwater. Nor is much attention given to the fact that animal waste from livestock farms produces toxins classified by the federal government as hazardous materials, or that so many of the kids fighting and dying in Iraq and Afghanistan first saw the ocean or flew in an airplane because a recruiter talked with them one day at their high schools.

We're not implying that no one is advocating for rural America; people are. Our concern is that those people expend far too much energy just telling the rest of the nation that they should be worried about the countryside's fate. The greatest challenge is getting people outside of the region to see that the place where "real Americans" dwell has any serious problems at all.[4] The time is long overdue for an awakening to the social and economic crisis in the Heartland.

And so, just as the Homestead Act, a sweeping piece of legislation, made the Heartland's communities rise out of the prairie more than a century ago, we believe an equally grand and visionary intervention is required to revive the region. Without action within our lifetimes, much of the Heartland will be abandoned, with more communities like Ellis succumbing to the destructive forces of neglect and decline. If, as a nation, we decide not to intervene, then we must accept a future with a myriad of social problems throughout the countryside, the spread of rural wastelands, and the unraveling of civic institutions such as churches and local schools. The economic, political, and social costs of allowing huge swaths of the countryside to decline in this manner are simply too extreme to comprehend.

The good news is that there are an abundance of ideas about how to fix rural America; the challenge is that too few Americans are aware we're at a critical point. The first step for dealing with the rural crisis, then, is to educate more Americans about the forces threatening these communities and why, as a nation, it should be a priority to invest in them. Karl Stauber, a former deputy undersecretary for rural development at the Department of Agriculture, in 2001 offered several reasons why it is in all of our interests to rebuild the Heartland. Among his ideas are the production of what he calls "decommodified food," such as high-quality organic products; the development of healthy, well-educated citizens; becoming a site for immigration; protecting and renewing the environment; and establishing what he terms "centers of innovation."[5] Former Iowa governor Tom Vilsack, the incoming secretary of the Department of Agriculture, told us in the winter of 2008 that the impetus for investment in the rural Heartland should be based on the notion that reimagining the Heartland will mean building an infrastructure to address the most serious problems facing the nation and the world. Because of the emerging demands for "local food production, sustainable agriculture, and renewable clean energy," there is a critical need for "investments in vigorous and robust rural communities." Vilsack concluded, "Leaders in government, business, or environmental advocacy would do well to fully commit to a new creative rural economy."[6]

It is useful to examine some of the main ideas that have been proffered as solutions to the hollowing-out problem, to what extent they can address the current crisis, and what this means for Ellis and for all other towns facing an uncertain future.

IF YOU BUILD IT, WILL THEY COME?

It is hard to escape the *Field of Dreams* parallels in the proposals that stem from the creative-class thesis. The adaptation of the Richard Florida framework for building creative cities a la Silicon Valley or the Research Triangle in North Carolina has captured the imagination of many policy makers. The idea influenced and inspired governors and prompted investment in economic infrastructure and development, as witnessed with the state of Michigan's Cool Cities Initiative. The creative-class thesis prioritizes the building and marketing of amenities to attract the educated entrepreneurial members of the creative class.[7] What remains less clear is whether the widespread development of local amenities can bear the fruit that many hope for and, in particular, whether creative towns can be conjured in places that have been largely emptying out. Can small towns in nonmetropolitan areas attract the creative class, and, if they can, what can this do for local economies?

The simple answer to the attraction question is, we believe, yes. The United States Department of Agriculture's Economic Research Service from 2007 finds strong evidence of the creative class in rural areas; this included people who are business owners, scientists, engineers, designers, and artists. Moreover, the presence of these people was "associated with measures of creativity, such as patent awards and technology adoption, and with growth in jobs during 1990–2004."[8] So talent poaching may be a more viable option than attracting a new factory to encourage local economic growth. However, as we have seen in our accounts of the Returners, luring educated, creative people to small towns is no easy feat. Bike paths and entertainment zones, in themselves, will not persuade significant numbers of professional-class workers to leave the undeniable economic benefits of metro centers and relocate to small towns.

Just 11 percent of all nonmetro counties qualify as creative-class regions, and two-thirds of all creative-class counties are in metropolitan areas. In other words, most creative-class counties are in urban areas, not rural ones. Still, every state has a smattering of nonmetro "creative counties," and Iowa's Jefferson County is a prime example of an area that is bustling because of the many migrants who have settled there in the past two decades. Today, the county is home to more than one hundred software-development companies, proof of the creative-class prescription for knowledge, economic growth, and positive change.[9] Most nonmetro creative counties are found in New England and in the Mountain West states such as Colorado, Wyoming, and Utah.[10] It should come as little surprise that the so-called New Heartland rural areas disproportionately benefit from the creative-class influx. Indeed, a report by the Brookings Institution released in August 2008 chronicled the rapid economic expansion of the southern intermountain states of Arizona, Colorado, Nevada, New Mexico, and Utah.[11]

But what is a net gain for the New Heartland is a net loss for the old one. The persistent and increasing inequality in the regional distribution of the creative class makes it difficult to see how Heartland small towns will compete with areas in the West that have more abundant outdoor amenities such as mountains, hiking trails, and ski resorts. Most places—Ellis, Iowa, included—will never be Aspen, and the slickest marketing campaign and the most beautiful parks and libraries will never change that fact. Having great amenities or an institutional magnet such as a university enhances the chances of attracting knowledge-economy innovators, but the competition for such workers is intense. Investing in technologies such as DSL and the Internet or improving existing amenities is probably a good idea for all small towns to enhance the quality of life and create a sort of fertilizer for helping local entrepreneurial opportunities grow. But although the creative-class solution is part of the answer, it is not the panacea that so many have hoped it would be.

RETOOLING SMALL TOWNS
FOR A GLOBAL ECONOMY

Though chasing the creative class seems fundamentally flawed in terms of its potential to address the overall hollowing out of the Heartland, the central insight that towns must be able to adapt to the modern postindustrial economy resonates. Small towns must wean themselves from the traditional economic mainstays of agriculture and manufacturing. Reimagining the Heartland boils down to (re)building microeconomies and providing the opportunities to sustain schools and communities currently devastated by aging demographics and out-migration. The recession that is bearing down on the nation's economy will undoubtedly accelerate the regional decline. Already Iowa has started to shed manufacturing jobs, as it routinely does in a recession. A report indicated that the state lost twenty-four hundred factory jobs in the first nine months of 2008, and further layoffs are widely anticipated.[12]

Small towns such as Ellis remain particularly vulnerable because they depend on one or two big employers. Indeed, at this writing, there are unsettling rumors that Tantech is about to begin layoffs that will be more severe and sustained than ever before. The restructuring that comes in such an economy should be a chance to retool to become more competitive. Rather than fighting globalization, the Heartland must come to terms with the new reality.[13] In the words of the journalist and author Richard Longworth, "There is no place in a globalized world for the small town and the family farm."[14] Although this is an extreme and deliberately provocative statement, it forces a discussion of what steps small towns must make to thrive in a global economy, and what role they can realistically have in the new world economic order.

The socioeconomic and political infrastructures of the Midwest have been ill equipped to deal with a global economy. Schools cannot prepare students adequately, and workers have been slow to retool themselves in response to the demands of the postindustrial economy. That huge factory farms have displaced the family farm and that manufacturing in the Midwest has been eroded during the past few decades have served to economically marginalize many areas—the net result being that the Midwest generally, and small towns in particular, fall further behind. Though Longworth sees out-migration as a consequence rather than a cause of this process, when the brain drain is added to the mix, the prospects for small towns look bleak.[15]

Longworth advocates the development of a regional identity and Midwestern think tanks that will generate new ideas and a focus on issues common to the region. He also calls for a wholesale renovation of education and training that will include a rebuilding of the public school system and an increase in cooperation among institutions of higher learning to enhance resources and eliminate duplication. Finally, Longworth argues that the physical and digital infrastructure should be upgraded to enhance networking and promote productivity. Collectively, these measures will enhance cooperation among states similarly affected by globalization and increase the opportunities and capacity to compete in the global marketplace.

There is much to admire in the scope of Longworth's analysis.

However, his prescription for renewal may ensure that there are regional winners and losers, with the latter more likely to be the small towns that find it difficult to compete with larger regional centers. What Longworth underemphasizes in the sweep of his analysis is that there are places in the Midwest that have fared well in the global economy and that, by and large, these places are in and around large metropolitan areas. Though it is not inconceivable that small towns would benefit from the changes that he advocates, we would caution that the bulk of the benefit would go to larger conurbations. Timothy Collins, assistant director of the Illinois Institute for Rural Affairs at Western Illinois University, argues that Longworth needs to "consider a parallel strategy, one that fosters *sustainable* smaller places and sees them as *viable players in the global economy*. The continued demise of rural areas and small cities is *not inevitable*."[16] Collins then outlines an additional set of measures that address the globalization challenge for small towns and rural communities, including creating incentives and opportunities for rural communities, enhancing links between nonmetropolitan areas and larger urban areas, fostering small-business development, and reskilling displaced workers.[17]

We certainly recognize that small towns must be able to flourish in a global economy, and based on our conversations with Stayers and Returners, we acknowledge an urgent need to revamp the rural educational system (namely, in its chronic underinvestment in its non-college-bound students) to offer opportunities for people to acquire new skills, along the lines of the equalizing of opportunities we discussed earlier. In line with these basic educational reforms targeted toward the Returners and Stayers as much as the Achievers, we echo the suggestions of calling for policy to be coordinated across the region, as well as for upgrading the digital technology infrastructure in small towns.

In 2008, Iowa Governor Chet Culver called on his state to become a serious competitor in the drive to create a green economy,
and he proposed a plan to cover one thousand acres of the state with
solar panels, which would generate enough energy to power more
than 110,000 homes. Governor Culver noted that Iowa gets as much
sun as Hawaii and that his brother had recently called Des Moines
"the Santa Monica of the Midwest."[18] Now that President Obama
has called for green technology to play a central role in the push for
energy independence, why shouldn't small towns, and those who
live there, benefit? The expected green energy boom—combined
with a push for sustainable agriculture—promises areas for potential growth and innovation in nonmetropolitan America. Indeed,
wind farms already have been constructed in Iowa, Kansas, Wyoming, and other states in the plains. But new technology development and entrepreneurship require an educated, technology-savvy,
young labor force, and so education and training must be re-
envisioned to meet this challenge.

However, like the creative-class solution, the "adapting for globalization" argument founders when we come to terms with the
critical shortage of educated workers in the region. The Heartland's
growing educational deficits will continue to be one of the most
serious roadblocks for the region if it is to take advantage of coming
opportunities in the globalized marketplace. Simply put, globalization readiness—without human- and digital-capital investments in
the countryside's labor forces—means that better equipped metropolitan areas will always have the upper hand in attracting and
developing new industries. Therefore, it is critical that economic
development in rural areas proceed hand in hand with digital investments and human-capital development. Simply put, prosperity
cannot come to this region without better preparing the Stayers and
Returners for biotech and technology jobs; keeping a greater share
of the Achievers home; luring more in-migrants (possibly through

immigration); and building an infrastructure, supported through cutting-edge digital technology, that reduces the economic costs of conducting business far from center cities.

MODERN-DAY ELLIS ISLANDS: THE UNEASY PATH
TO INTEGRATION IN THE HEARTLAND

When then-governor Tom Vilsack declared he wanted to make Iowa the "Ellis Island of the Midwest" soon after taking office in 1998, his vision was far from popular among his fellow Iowans. Undaunted, Governor Vilsack appointed a Strategic Planning Council to coordinate these efforts. The central idea was simple: create incentives to attract skilled immigrants to the state as an antidote to the declining and aging population in many small towns. In some ways, Governor Vilsack was responding to developments already happening in parts of the state. New settlements of Mexicans and Central Americans mushroomed around meat-processing plants: Postville, Storm Lake, and Lexington had become de facto immigrant enclaves. Governor Vilsack hoped the state's involvement in immigration would make the transition more structured, planned, and orderly, but the immigrants he most wanted to attract were engineers, computer scientists, and doctors, not just farm and factory workers.

Part of the Vilsack plan was the designation of Iowa as an immigration enterprise zone, so as to be exempt from federal quotas, with the express goal of bringing in close to half a million workers to fill positions in agribusiness and manufacturing that the declining and aging native population could not. Formulating an open-door policy for immigrants would be an effort to "encourage a smooth transition for bringing skilled workers and their families to Iowa from other countries."[19]

But before the governor could implement his original plan, stricter immigration policies in the wake of 9/11 essentially killed the effort. Vilsack remained committed to rapidly integrating

Iowa's new workers, and so he developed the "New Iowans Pilot Project," which proposed the creation of three model communities that would become "a positive model for immigration . . . that will be [follow]ed by other communities across the state."[20] The communities of Fort Dodge, Marshalltown, and Mason City were selected based on a number of criteria, such as the availability of economic opportunities and local infrastructure—housing, schools, and services—and the willingness of local leaders to participate in the project.

Though these were not the "skilled workers" that the New Iowans initiative ideally intended to bring into the state, there was growing recognition that new immigrants, even ones with modest educations and skills, could be a vital source of future growth and development. And yet, given the newcomers' lack of English and limited education, the need to promote integration would be singularly important. Iowa is one of the least racially and ethnically diverse states in the country, and the resources that help immigrants in urban areas of other states have never really existed there. Those inclined to welcome the immigrants understood that the process of easing their transition would be crucial.

Almost immediately, several cities and small towns in the region produced Spanish-language "welcome" videos, sponsored ESL courses, and worked on efforts to foster integration and tolerance. University of Northern Iowa professor Mark Grey, who has written extensively about immigration in Iowa and evaluated the New Iowans program, founded the Iowa Center on Immigrant Leadership and Immigration in 1999 with a mission to guide and prepare "Iowa communities and businesses as they accommodate immigrant and refugee newcomers living and working in Iowa."[21] Grey's program consults with communities as they prepare for in-migration; it educates civic and community leaders on the needs of these new populations and does so with a "strong appreciation for the critical role newcomers play in ensuring the long-term social and economic vi-tality of Iowa's businesses and communities."[22] Grey's consortium was not the only one calling on Iowans to welcome newcomers. In the spring of 2002, a group of Catholic nuns in the Upper Mis-sissippi Valley area embarked on a public-awareness campaign to promote an understanding of the plight of immigrants and to foster acceptance of the newcomers, at the same time that proponents of an English-only law sought to demonize them. The centerpiece of the nuns' campaign was a billboard that displayed a Polaroid picture of an extended Hispanic family: grandparents, parents, and four children, including a baby. Each member of the family is dressed smartly, as if for a formal occasion (perhaps the baby's baptism), and they gaze earnestly at the camera. On the right-hand side of the billboard is the caption "Welcome the Immigrant *You* Once Were!" The subtext of the message is clear: today's immigrants are no different from your family members who traveled by train and wagon to build a life in the prairie a hundred years ago. Hardwork-ing, religious, and devoted to family, they share your values.

However, even as these grassroots campaigns have gained some traction, the backlash against immigrants in Iowa and elsewhere has become even more energized and coordinated. Grey and his colleagues could see a swell of anti-immigrant sentiment grow-ing.[23] Political pragmatism compelled Governor Vilsack to sign an English-only bill into law. In response, critics charged that the gov-ernor had forsaken his earlier position on immigration because he was up for re-election and public opinion at the time opposed his pro-immigrant efforts. At the time, he said that though the bill was "not without controversy . . . [m]y hope is that we will look beyond the controversy and put politics behind us so we can focus on our commitments and responsibility to improve education for all our children."[24]

In February 2005, not long after Governor Vilsack abandoned

his plans for immigrants, he redoubled his efforts to lure Achievers back to the state during the "Come Back to Iowa, Please" campaign.[25] In the end, it didn't matter about the English-only law, because the immigrants kept coming.[26] At the same time, more and more food processors began employing large numbers of immigrant workers at plants that were increasingly located in isolated rural counties. By deskilling and mechanizing all parts of the production process, the food industry was cutting labor costs and maximizing profits.[27] Relocating factories from large urban areas to smaller towns in the Heartland—which brings companies closer to the source of their raw materials and reduces costs at their facilities—became another way to increase profit margins. Many places chosen as sites for agribusiness plants have an aging and inadequate workforce, and so companies have, in many cases, recruited immigrants to be the surplus labor pool they need to operate there.[28] The results of these changes in the food-processing industry have transformed the racial and ethnic composition of communities and put downward pressure on wages.[29] What were solid lower-middle-class jobs a generation ago have now become barely subsistence. In the immigrants' search for a better life, their arrival appeared, to many longtime residents, to be the reason for growing economic uncertainty. Immigrants were the perfect scapegoats. It didn't matter that corporations were exploiting the new employees horribly or that the native white workers would never take $6.25 an hour to slaughter chickens. The only truth that mattered was that the agribusinesses' reliance on immigrant workers was driving down wages.

During the 2004 presidential campaign season, a group called the Coalition for the Future American Worker purchased airtime for an ad featuring an inflatable dummy getting struck over and over again. In the voiceover, the narrator wonders aloud, "How much longer can Iowa workers be the punching bags for greedy corporations and politicians? First, meatpackers replaced Iowans with thousands of foreign workers. Next, wages were cut almost in half. Now, politicians want new laws to import millions more foreign workers and give amnesty to illegal aliens. Tell the candidates no more foreign workers and no amnesty for millions here illegally." Some stations pulled the spot after a barrage of complaints, including from the Iowa Federation of Labor, but the sentiment expressed in the ad was indicative of how many people felt about immigration.

States like Iowa depend on agribusiness for jobs and revenue, and even if they did decide to try to regulate the industry, there is a danger that companies will simply relocate to states where officials will not ask too many questions. So wages remain low, and both legal and undocumented workers flock to fill the poor-paying, unskilled, and sometimes dangerous jobs. The result for immigrants is what *Wall Street Journal* columnist Thomas Frank describes as becoming captives of the meatpacking archipelago, where workers, some of whom are underage and undocumented, are routinely (and sometimes illegally) forced to work long hours for low pay and few benefits.[30] A second development has been the federal government's crackdown on undocumented immigrants, which came to a head with the May 12, 2008, raid on Agriprocessors in Postville, Iowa. Reputedly the largest such raid in United States history, it saw 389 people arrested and scores of others seeking sanctuary in St. Brigid's Catholic Church in the town. The raid, executed by the Immigrant and Customs Enforcement wing of the Department of Homeland Security, was said to be part of a larger effort to enforce immigration laws, an effort that also included several hundred arrests at Pilgrim's Pride poultry plants in five states. By the middle of October 2008, fifty of the people arrested at Postville had been deported and another fifty were awaiting deportation; the remainder of the "adult" detainees—several were juveniles—remained incarcerated, most of them charged with using fraudulent Social Security numbers.

These megaraids and their aftermath illustrate very clearly the absurdity of the present immigration policy. Many of the arrested workers have lived in their adopted towns for more than a decade and have, in that time, settled down and started families. Most of the children of these undocumented immigrants are American citizens, and groups such as the nuns described earlier have worked to reunite family members separated by the raids. In a radio commercial calling for immigration reform, Franciscan sister Hilary Mullany from Clinton, Iowa, pleads with her fellow Iowans: "Most Americans have compassion for suffering people. Yet some turn a cold shoulder to the anguish of undocumented families torn apart by the recent federal raids. Like Scandinavian, European, and Asian people before them, today's immigrants come seeking only freedom and a better life for their children. Contact your legislators and candidates today to urge immediate action for comprehensive immigration reform." Sister Mullany did not even mention the economic burden on taxpayers and small towns resulting from punitive anti-immigrant efforts; the Postville raid cost American taxpayers an estimated $5.2 million.[31]

Immigration can be a transformative force for small towns and depopulating rural areas, but it is one that is unpredictable, controversial, and subject to the eddies of political whim. As it currently exists in the Heartland, immigration is too unstable to be a reliable solution to hollowing out; however, with the right reforms at the federal level and planning at the state and local levels, it can be an important part of future planning and policy. Lewiston, Maine, has shown how, with planning, ingenuity, and the diversion of resources, a sudden influx of newcomers can be successfully integrated and provide a boost to the city's overall well-being.[32]

ECONOMIC GARDENING: HOMETOWN
COMPETITIVENESS AND FREE LAND PROGRAMS

As the states that have been most affected by hollowing out have ramped up their campaigns to entice young people to stay or return, ranging from the IOWA *life*|Changing campaign to the Michigan Cool Cities Initiative, some small towns across the Heartland have taken their own bold steps to take control of their fate. As with the larger state programs, these efforts have centered either on bolstering the local economy or on providing amenities that increase the attractiveness of the town. Ellis, for example, has struggled but so far managed to keep much of its local economic base intact. There are still enough decent-paying blue-collar jobs and a smattering of professional openings to maintain the short-term viability of the town, even as the demographic threat of an aging population looms. But it is uncertain how the worldwide economic crisis will affect towns like Ellis and their fragile economies. What is clear is that the popular tactic of luring even medium-sized companies to small towns with incentives, tax breaks, and the promise of an eager workforce, a practice often referred to as "elephant hunting," is ineffective for most small towns. As a result, many towns have turned their attention away from an economic big score in the hope of arresting decline one family at a time.

The counterpoint to elephant hunting is often called "economic gardening," and the focus is on planting multiple seeds for local growth in the hope that some will bear fruit. Some of the components of economic gardening can be grouped under the banner of the Home Town Competitiveness (HTC) program, which was developed in 2002 by the joint efforts of the Heartland Center for Leadership Development, the Nebraska Community Foundation, and the Center for Rural Entrepreneurship in Lincoln, Nebraska.[33]

The program is self-described as a "come back/give back approach to rural community building," and it seeks to go beyond the "tunnel vision" attitude toward economic development by focusing on four pillars of development: leadership, youth, entrepreneurship, and charitable assets. The goal is to "increase the capacity of residents to improve and sustain their community." The youth pillar is designed to "support and enhance the idea of adults and youth working together to create opportunities for youth to stay in or return to the community."[34] Entrepreneurship seeks to identify and nurture entrepreneurial talent and provide support for business development. Increasing charitable assets is touted as a way to build a community endowment that can be used to bolster efforts to increase competitiveness. In many ways, the program contains elements that can be adapted to equalize the investments in different types of young people. Though it seems implicit that the Achievers are sought more than Stayers or Returners, there is every reason to believe that a community endowment and encouragement of entrepreneurship can be used to train, skill, and invest in Stayers, while also providing incentives for the college-educated members of the creative class to return.

At the heart of economic gardening is the familiar impulse to keep the best talent at home or at least to get them back after they finish their education. One strategy is to give them land to build on, which is precisely what about a dozen small towns in Kansas have done. Operating as independent entities or as consortiums, these towns are part of the so-called Free Land in Kansas program, started in 2003. Ellsworth, the county seat of a central Kansas county by the same name, has been at the forefront of this program, the aim of which is to arrest decades of population loss and, in the words of one newspaper report, "expand the tax base, keep schools from closing and preserve a way of life."[35] The county, through the Smoky Hill Development Corporation, runs the "Welcome Home Program," in which four towns offer free residential lots to encourage families to locate within the county. The free lots are offered contingent on bank preapproval and on the proviso that families meet a number of deadlines: they must sign a contractor within six months, break ground within a year, and take occupancy of the dwelling within twenty-four months. In return, the towns of Ellsworth, Holyrood, Kanopolis, and Wilson will give families an approximately fifteen thousand-square-foot lot on which to build a home with a poured concrete foundation. Each town has additional enticements for families planning to relocate there. For instance, Ellsworth offers free water and sewer hookups, a waiver of the building permit fee, and a family golf pass, a family swimming-pool pass, or paid recreation fees for a year. Ellsworth County offers a down payment assistance program for families who enroll their children in the local public schools and commit to keep them there for three years. The assistance comes in the form of $1,000 for the first child and $250 for each subsequent child enrolled, and it is paid at the time of settlement.

Though Kansas has taken the lead in the free-land concept, the idea has spread to other states, and small towns such as Marne, in western Iowa, have adopted their own version of it. Marne has a modest goal of boosting its population from 149 to 200 and hopes especially to attract families with young children. Similar programs have mushroomed in Minnesota (Hendrum), Wyoming (Chugwater), and North Dakota (Crosby), all with the stated intention of luring newcomers. Initially, at least, the free-land programs generated a great deal of interest, and many available lots were snapped up quickly. What is less clear is how successful this program will be with time, because it is essentially a long-term bet, and there is always the worry that families may not settle in or that they may move again when the free golf passes expire. Still, as of the summer of 2005, the town of Marquette in Kansas, which has a population of around five hundred, had given away eighty lots and begun developing an additional twenty acres.[36] The short-term result is that the population of Marquette has increased by a third, and enrollment at the school has been boosted. Reinvigorating the school—described as the "driving issue" for Marquette—is vital for the survival of any small town, and it is a first step in arresting the hollowing-out process.

Not all settlers moving to small towns are families with school-age children.[37] Some are retirees who are attracted to the Midwest for a variety of reasons, including abundant land and the many leisure opportunities. Indeed, many of the nonmetropolitan counties that have maintained their populations have done so because of the leisure activities that bolster local economies and attract new people. One study found that the population growth in the 12 percent of nonmetropolitan counties identified as recreational has consistently exceeded that in other nonmetropolitan areas. More important, the bulk of this growth has accrued from in-migration.[38] Whereas the towns in Ellsworth County can trumpet their proximity to larger urban areas such as Salina and Hays,[39] and the city of Ellsworth itself boasts that it is only seven miles south of Interstate 70, other areas, such as Atwood in northwest Kansas, rely upon "abundant deer, pheasant, quail and wild turkeys"[40] to tempt retirees who value the outdoors. Most of the Iowans who returned or stayed told us that their idea of a great weekend was to go hunting and fishing, so there is a synergy between leisure seekers and those remaining in the countryside.

That this scaled-down local version of the thrice-failed New Homestead Act[41] has initially succeeded in several places and prompted a legion of copycat ventures perhaps is a testament to the existence of strong vital signs for some towns. But there are those who would caution against believing that these piecemeal efforts at growth will work everywhere. Just as there are winners and losers with respect to large metropolitan areas striving to be the next destination for the creative class, some small towns will benefit and others will lose from free-land initiatives. Regardless of whether they are successful, these efforts underscore the fact that many small towns, including Ellis, have not given up their futures and refuse to believe that they might not exist one day.

IS SMALL-TOWN DECLINE INEVITABLE?

More than two decades ago, Deborah and Frank Popper, professors of geography and environmental studies, advanced the thesis that the Great Plains, which had always been the site of boom-and-bust cycles, was entering an inevitable decline and that rural areas would continue to depopulate. This, combined with overgrazing, overplowing, and overirrigating, would rob the region of soil, water, people, and community.[42] The answer to such an inevitable decline, argued the Poppers, was to return much of the Great Plains to its original state—a Buffalo Commons, which, they explained, would be a "metaphor for a fresh way of thinking about the region's land use."[43] Though the Poppers have been largely right about the population trends in many nonmetropolitan counties,[44] their prescription for renewal, turning the "ailing plains into a vast . . . venue for bison and prairie restoration, ecotourism and niche marketing of bison products" has been wildly controversial, yet it has increasingly gained in popularity.[45] Although the idea began as a metaphor, it has led to some actual changes in the plains states, and some of these have affected small towns in positive, sustaining ways. For instance, the Poppers pointed out that growing numbers of farmers have "found their land more valuable as habitat than farmland . . . and Native Americans, whose populations are increasing in the rural Great Plains as the white populations diminish, are actively restoring buffalo on their reservations."[46] As time has passed, and the Poppers' initial nihilistic assessment of the future of small towns and rural homesteads has been tempered, they no longer see the solution as a federal government–sponsored relocation program, but rather as something that is decentralized, locally controlled, and tailored to suit the emerging exigencies of the rapidly depopulating nonmetropolitan counties in many states. It is hardly surprising that North Dakota, the state that has experienced the most devastating population losses, is where the Poppers' ideas have gained the most purchase. In fact, Frank Popper described North Dakota as "the leader" in promoting the Commons idea.[47]

As an ecological and, indeed, practical solution to the emptying out of many plains regions and the lack of agricultural viability in many rural places, the Buffalo Commons idea is sound. Yet the initial reaction to the Poppers' ideas was so severe that they required police protection at talks they gave on the topic. Certainly, there is a knee-jerk reaction to the gloomy forecast of an end to the small town on the plains and the reversion of the land to a more natural verdant state. People are attached to the idea of small towns, and there is the agribusiness imperialism of land use to contend with as well. The Poppers believe that many of the efforts to bring new people to the plains, with offers of free land, for instance, are doomed to failure. Frank Popper has been quoted as saying that "Americans, on the whole, don't see the Great Plains as a very attractive place. They will go to places with trout streams and mountains. They don't go to western Kansas."[48] Moreover, the Poppers believe that such efforts merely forestall the inevitable, and certainly the weight of demographic evidence on the natural population decline in many rural counties tends to support their claim. But perhaps there is a compromise position that does not see the situation as hopeless yet recognizes the essential truths and promise of the Buffalo Commons prescription.

WHAT DOES THIS MEAN FOR ELLIS?

The policies and programs for saving small towns run the gamut. Small towns can chase the creative class by developing local amenities, or try to lure back Achievers with loan-forgiveness programs or free land. They can be part of a regional economic plan to retool for the global economy, or they can elephant-hunt agribusiness or manufacturing and cope with the accompanying influx of immigrants that many of these plants bring. Small towns can be part of the drive to rethink farming and move toward agricultural niche marketing and the Buffalo Commons. There are elements of all these prescriptions that are worth retaining, but individually and collectively, these solutions fall somewhat short of what needs to be done to stop debilitating population loss in the Heartland. One of the major reasons for this is the failure to see small towns as ground zero for hollowing out, a point that was forcefully driven home during our time in Ellis and evident in conversations we had with its young adults. In their hearts, the key institutional actors in small towns are aware that what they do is flawed and inherently self-defeating, yet they are slow to embrace the kind of thinking that will help them face the challenges ahead.

Therefore, we probably shouldn't have been surprised that the high school's principal, George Herdemann, and his school board were aware of the key role they play in the hollowing-out process, yet could not envision themselves doing anything differently. After all, preparing the most talented young people to leave and succeed has traditionally been the modus operandi of small towns, and a vital part of the town's civic pride is from the collective satisfaction of knowing that the young person you watched mature, and whom you might have coached or taught to play an instrument, has succeeded elsewhere. But what was once the hallmark of a vibrant small town—helping Achievers leave—is now the driving force behind the hollowing-out process. Certainly there are more opportunities for Achievers, especially young women, than there were three decades ago, and so the siphoning-off of the educated and talented is perhaps more efficient and debilitating than at any time in the past. But crucially, the local economy that sustained generations of Stayers and Returners has started to come apart at the seams. The rise of agribusiness and the attendant decline of the family farm, exemplified by the disappearance of barns from the rural landscape,[49] have utterly changed agriculture in the Heartland. And the parallel shifts in manufacturing in the postindustrialization era have, in turn, remade the other bellwether of the Heartland economy. Fewer people work in agriculture, and although many Stayers still have jobs in industry, those jobs pay less and have fewer benefits than they did a generation ago.

What happens at the level of the small town is mirrored and magnified and spreads. The chain of events set in motion reverberates and has consequences for the state and the Midwest as a whole. Simply put, if you start preparing people to leave when they are in their teens, why should you be surprised when many of them migrate away from their home states once they finish college? It is impossible to groom someone to leave and then, after what is, for many, a decade-long process, do an about-face and entice them to stay. A few will choose to return, but many more will follow the well-worn swaths that the brain drain has carved through the Heartland. So what is to be done at this level of the problem?

We recognize that the careful cultivation of the "cream of the crop" is probably not going to change, and we would argue that it probably shouldn't. After all, it would be unconscionable to deny young people a chance to excel and use their talents. We would caution, however, that the Ellis case illustrates that this is not a perfect meritocracy and that, in fact, there are subtle class advantages that accrue to elite and influential families in small towns that should not be ignored.

But given that the meritocracy is imperfect and unlikely to change, the Ellis case shows us that what is not happening with respect to the Stayers and Returners is perhaps a key part of the solution to the hollowing-out process. As Achievers are imbued with the resources and support that ease their transition away from Ellis, there is a fundamental underinvestment in those who stay and many who return. Though this may not have mattered in the heyday of the agri-industrial economy, when blue-collar jobs in farming or manufacturing were plentiful and could sustain a family, it is critically important today. This is because jobs for those with few skills are scarce in the current economy and, if available, pay less in real terms and have fewer benefits than similar positions did in previous generations. The postindustrial economy demands technical skill sets that need to be continually updated to keep up with the rapid pace of scientific progress. We found that many of the Stayers and Returners we interviewed not only lacked these skills but lamented the fact that they had not been able to acquire them in their schooling.

An obvious first step that many small towns can take is to equalize their investment across different groups of young people and to tie education and training for Stayers more closely to the demands of the modern global economy, which places a premium on technical computer-based skills. One way to develop the skills of those not bound for baccalaureate programs is to use the existing community college infrastructure, which we believe to be underutilized in many rural areas. For instance, there are several community colleges within easy commuting distance of Ellis, and they could be easily tapped to provide bridge programs for young people during and after high school. Already schools such as Hawkeye Community College in Waterloo, Iowa, and Riverland in Austin, Minnesota, have programs for high school juniors and seniors to earn college credits, and Hawkeye offers a Career Academies program in which high school students can learn about careers in manufacturing, health care, and information technology.[50] We would recommend that high schools in small towns avail themselves of these programs, and we would also suggest widening the scope of these programs to offer credit and certification to non-college-bound high school students. Too often, the emphasis, even at the community college level, is on those students who are likely to pursue an academic track, not on those who pursue other routes. But the latter group sorely needs the skills to be able to succeed in the modern economy.

Already there are signs that policy makers are thinking about the role of community colleges in regional development initiatives in the Heartland. The state of Kansas, for example, has recognized that retooling community colleges to meet the demands of the modern economy is a priority. The state's Department of Commerce oversees a Working Solutions Fund that disburses money directly to community colleges to stimulate innovation and curriculum change to address workforce needs. A recent example of this program is a grant for $155,000 that the state gave to Cloud County Community College, in north-central Kansas, in 2008 to "expand its Wind Energy Technology program and increase Kansas's capacity for wind energy production."[51] The funding is designed to provide "staff and equipment for its Associate of Applied Science degree program in Wind Energy Technology, the only such program in Kansas and one of just five nationwide."[52] Though wind energy is still an underdeveloped area of America's overall energy program, it appears there will be renewed interest and focus on this issue in future government policy.[53] A more traditional grant is the $141,050 that Garden City Community College, in western Kansas, received in June 2008 to expand its welding training program. This is specifically to train workers for Palmer Manufacturing, Tank Inc., and Tyson Fresh Foods, all of which have plants in the area.

In an article on the rural brain drain, Georgeanne Artz, a rural economist from the University of Missouri, makes a number of recommendations for "plugging the drain."[54] At the heart of Artz's analysis is her insistence on the need for nonmetropolitan and rural counties to attract people with human capital (education and skills) because, she argues, "higher levels of human capital are associated with higher levels of income, increased productivity and economic growth." She points out that most of the efforts at retaining college graduates or attracting them back have focused on recent gradu- ates who mostly flock to metropolitan areas because of the higher returns on education found there, and because this is rational be- havior, we should not try to stop them. Instead, Artz insists, efforts should focus on attracting "experienced college-educated workers" because their preferences for where to live "may change with age." As with some of the poster children for the IOWA *life*|Changing campaign, these would-be High-Flyers would return for quality- of-life reasons. The central thrust of this argument is that policy makers and small towns should be concerned with the supply of *all* educated workers, not just those with newly minted degrees. Al- though it is a cogent point, we believe this overlooks a fundamental opportunity to raise the human-capital level of those who stay. In other words, we agree with analyses that place human capital front and center of any local economic growth, but it is crucial to recog- nize that there are sources of human capital other than Achievers. Part of the solution must be not only to change the prevailing way of investing in young people but also in coordinated efforts to raise overall levels of human capital.

A second step will be to awaken the country to the serious chal- lenges facing rural America and link a national call to move to sustainable agriculture and green energy technology to preparing the rural Heartland for the global marketplace. This call to arms will come with an expectation of not doing business as usual. Educational programs will need to be revamped so that the next generation of workers will have more options than simply following their parents into jobs at Deere. As noted, traditional blue-collar jobs that once expanded the middle class simply do not exist for today's workers, and, more important, the next generation must be trained for the realities of the new marketplace. Every young person who completes high school must be proficient in computer technologies, and for those not headed to college, high school curricula should be modeled after the most successful community college programs for accounting, business, nursing and medical technology (both areas experiencing shortages of qualified workers in Iowa), and computer science. Instead of preparing high school students for conventional four-year college curricula, education should be transformed to funnel young people into vocational and preprofessional training that will fill the holes in the countryside's labor force. It is dangerous and misguided to fund and operate rural high schools with the primary goal of getting the academically oriented students to college and assuming that the non-college-bound will somehow get a job on their own.

A third step for many small towns will be to manage immigration in ways that promote local growth and reduce intergroup tensions. Immigration can be a solution to the short- and long-term viability of many small towns in the Heartland, but only if there is a fundamental policy shift and if common mistakes are avoided. Several studies have shown that so-called Hispanic boomtowns can transform moribund local economies and inject new life into once dying places.[55] Almost two-thirds of the growth in Iowa's population during the 1990s was attributable to immigration, mostly from Hispanics, and in some places the increase in the Latino population

was tenfold.[56] Although there is an immediate boost to the population and local economy, there are also problems that accompany
such change.

Research by Domenico Parisi and Daniel Lichter shows that
Hispanic boomtowns are highly residentially segregated, which
does not augur well for assimilation into the wider community.[57]
The authors further warn that if past experience of urban racial and
ethnic segregation is anything to go by, one possible outcome is for
natives to engage in rural white flight, or the rapid change itself
can cause housing values to drop precipitously and crime rates to
increase, further exacerbating intergroup relations.[58] Policy makers and community leaders ought to be very concerned about how
these developments might lead to the expansion of rural ghettoes,
with the serious challenges they bring.[59] When you add to the mix
the low wages paid to immigrant workers, it becomes very clear
that immigration is not the straightforward panacea some think
it to be.

Immigration can be the foundation of population growth in the
region; however, we cannot underscore strongly enough the importance of overseeing immigration as we assimilate and educate
workers and prepare them for a globalized economy. We must understand that preventing the rise of rural ghettoes must go hand
in hand with immigration policy reform on the national level. We
believe what is needed is a guest-worker program and pathways
to legal status for longtime residents. Also, at a federal and state
level, there has to be willingness to regulate the industries that
most commonly employ immigrants. Even as Agriprocessors in
Postville was in the national headlines for the massive raid and the
large number of illegal immigrants working there, the poor, unsafe,
and exploitative working conditions at the plant provided another
compelling facet to the case, and the company had been the subject
of sanctions from the Iowa Department of Labor Services for viola-

tions of safety rules on numerous occasions. While Agriprocessors is an outlier in terms of its malfeasance, the larger point is that working conditions in the agribusiness sector must be improved as a matter of urgency. We would recommend tighter oversight by state and federal regulatory bodies, far beyond the voluntary compliance policy[60] that is currently pursued to one that mandates compulsory safety training, permits organized labor to represent workers and bargain with employers for better wages and benefits,[61] and generally improves working conditions for all in this sector. These efforts would benefit not only immigrants but also native workers, and they might also make these jobs more attractive to Stayers.

There are other pitfalls that must be avoided if immigration is to be an effective tool against hollowing out. As the immigrant population booms in many small towns, newcomers are largely segregated from the native population.[62] As we have seen during the past several decades, the same process of segregation in our urban centers has led to the social isolation of minority populations, exacerbated inequality, and contributed to the rise of an underclass.[63] Though on a lesser scale, the same segregation in small towns, if unchecked, will have many of the same negative outcomes, and so if we are to learn anything from the travails of American cities, we should seek to avoid making the same mistakes in our small towns. Finally, states can also build on the efforts of the nonprofit organizations that have been working to improve on-the-ground attempts at integration by allocating more resources to these efforts and crafting a public-service campaign that builds upon the messages promoted by previous campaigns, such as the theme of minimizing difference found in the billboard and radio spots produced by the Catholic nuns.[64]

If Iowa and similar states are to increase their population by creating immigrant enterprise zones and opening up opportunities for more skilled, English-speaking immigrants to help fill the shortages of doctors, scientists, and engineers, federal policy for immigrants must change. Moreover, easing integration and formulating a clear, standardized policy will eliminate the costly illegal-immigrant interdiction efforts and prevent the divisive and reactionary responses we have witnessed in places such as Hazleton, Pennsylvania.[65] In Iowa and throughout the rural Heartland, there are stories of communities that have dealt with immigration effectively. Successful programs should be widely supported and expanded to communities in the process of the same transitions.

A final step that small towns such as Ellis can take is to capitalize on the proposed economic stimulus and infrastructure plan that President Obama has put forth. Although, as of this writing, the plan has yet to assume a firm shape, the intimations are that the federal government may initiate a public-works program as ambitious as the New Deal. The I-35W Mississippi River bridge collapse in Minneapolis on August 1, 2007, tragically highlighted the crumbling state of the nation's infrastructure, and in the frantic work since by surveyors around the country it is apparent that there is an immediate need for investment in bridges, roads, and physical plants generally. This investment will be disseminated widely to the fifty states, and such decentralization offers hope that with a kick start of investment, the areas that are hollowing out can piggyback on this infusion to help remake their local economies. The other component of the new stimulus that is widely anticipated is investment in clean energy alternatives, and again, as we mentioned earlier, there is no reason that the Heartland cannot be an active participant in the drive for energy independence.

If the current uncertain economic climate promotes innovation, this offers a wonderful opportunity to reform farm policy to promote a wholesale reorganization of the food production system and to give a welcome boost to small farms. In a recent open letter to the incoming Obama administration, author Michael Pollan argues that "real reform of the food system may actually be possible for the first time in a generation."[66] A necessary first step in this reform is to limit the influence that agribusiness has had on farm policy since the Nixon administration. As Pollan and others have argued, the hegemony of industrial farming has produced farming monocultures of grain and meat, and this dependence on single products has meant the obliteration of crop diversity and the increased dependence on fossil fuels at every stage of the food chain. The consequences for individual health and the environment at large have been nothing short of catastrophic. Pollan says that it is not difficult to imagine a polyculture model of farming in the Midwest that would rotate grain crops with grass-fed beef in a way that will reduce the dependence on fossil fuels while sacrificing little in terms of production.[67] It will be daunting task for new Agriculture Secretary Tom Vilsack to change the way things are currently done in our food production system, but there are signs that such change has fertile ground upon which to grow.

First, there is a groundswell of people who are already seeking alternatives to commodified food in the form of organic and locally grown produce. Second, as Pollan argues, the federal government can easily redeploy the farming subsidies it already gives to encourage diversified farming, and the government can promote the use of organic produce for its sponsored nutrition programs. Finally, there is ample evidence in other countries, especially in Europe, of the viability of small farms and what they produce. This could be more than just niche marketing, and it would not be that much of a stretch to imagine Iowa as a "fantasy land of high-end cheese and beer and crazy-good steaks."[68] Certainly, the opportunity is there for the kind of reform in farm policy that would make this possible and fundamentally change the way we produce food. In addition, these reforms would create new opportunities for local economic development, particularly for the descendants of family farmers who, under existing conditions, have little incentive to stay on the land or remain in the region.

The economic stimulus appears to be a mixture of old and new economy initiatives, but the common theme is job creation. Moreover, the jobs being created will be sustaining ones and, as such, are essential building blocks in any recovery. The implications of the economic stimulus for stopping hollowing out are less clear, but we suspect that if the investment that will undoubtedly come to many small towns is integrated into a larger plan that includes many of the policies we suggest here, it could be a positive catalyst for profound changes in areas most affected by brain drain.

Whatever shape federal intervention and investment takes, the key is what happens at the level of the small town. If our conversations with the young men and women from Ellis have taught us anything, it is the inescapable truth that what unfolds in the social microcosm of each small town has important implications for how we tackle hollowing out. The root of the problem and the seeds of its solution are found in the way that each town prepares its young people, and in the institutions—employers, civic groups, Rotary clubs, schools, and colleges—that play a part in this effort. That process has to be remade as a first step before other policies can be adopted. To be sure, there are macroforces that shape the world in which Ellis youth come of age, and it would be foolish to deny the very real influence exerted by economic booms and slumps, globalization, or the mechanization of agriculture. But on a fundamental level, small towns can—if they question many of the taken-for-granted assumptions they have about who they should invest in and how—play a pivotal role in securing their own futures. They will need assistance and a bit of good fortune, but we believe that the demise of the small town in America's Heartland is far from inevitable. We are convinced that holding on to old ways of life, ignoring the problem, or passively refusing to act are simply not options. Why let small-town America die when, with a plan and a vision, it could be reborn and once again vital?

Acknowledgments

WE BEGAN TRAVELING TO IOWA IN February of 2001, and, after so many years devoted to this project, we have accumulated a multitude of debts.

First, we will be forever grateful that Frank Furstenberg, the director of the MacArthur Foundation's Network on Transitions to Adulthood, had the brilliant idea to study young people coming of age in rural America, and it is the combination of this vision and Frank's inveterate gambler's instinct in asking us to direct the Heartland Project. He helped us design the initial stages of the project, and at each successive phase he provided support, encouragement, and sage advice. We hope that this book rewards his faith in us and validates his instinct that there was something out there worth studying.

Under the auspices of the MacArthur Foundation, we joined a community of scholars who were as eager as we were to learn about our young Iowans. Conversations with Gordon Berlin, Mark Courtney, Sheldon Danziger, Connie Flanagan, Doug Hartmann, Jennifer Holdaway, Vonnie McLoyd, Wayne Osgood, Jean Rhodes, Cecilia Rouse, Ruben Rumbaut, Richard Settersten, Teresa Swartz, and Mary Waters were particularly valuable in all stages of re-search, analysis, and writing.

We owe a huge debt to the MacArthur Foundation itself, and although we had little direct contact with the program officers who have overseen the network program and its projects, we were never in doubt that what we were doing had the full and enthusiastic support of the foundation. We hope that we have repaid its generosity.

Barbara Ray, the network's communications director (and quint-essential Iowan Achiever), might well be considered this book's third author, and we thank her for the countless hours she has given us along with her ideas, editing, and citations. We are also heavily indebted to Patricia Miller, whose name is usually preceded by "the wonderful" and who, as the network's coordinator, made countless big and small things happen and took care of us and our Iowans in innumerable ways. Lisa Adams, our agent, has been a terrific advo-cate, wise editor, and enthusiastic cheerleader, and above all we are grateful for the fact that she kept encouraging us to imagine a book that was more than an ethnography of a single Iowa town.

Though we conducted nearly every interview recounted in this book, our Saint Joseph's University–based research assistants con-ducted some additional interviews, transcribed interviews, collected surveys, and helped analyze data. Special thanks to Bernadette Hall, Laura Napolitano, Joseph Doyle, Tina Armado, and Jessica Keating.

Several scholars of mature and recent vintage provided in-sightful comments and reactions to the very many drafts of chap-ters, and we especially acknowledge Frank Furstenberg, Kathryn Edin, Mitchell Stevens, Sharon Sassler, Connie Flanagan, Sheldon Danziger, Elizabeth Armstrong, and Nathan Fosse. Daniel Lich-ter gave us much-needed crash courses in rural sociology (but is not to blame for this book's remaining shortcomings), and William Kandel helped us tremendously with the maps. Audiences at Bryn Mawr College, New York University, the University of Chicago, and the University of Pennsylvania offered great insights on this project in various workshops and colloquia. David Karen and Marissa Golden, at Bryn Mawr College, provided Maria with the perfect home away from home when she held a visiting research associate appointment at the College's Social Science Research Center during her sabbatical year. Rutgers University and Saint Joseph's University both provided generous leaves that were crucial in the writing of this book, and we are thankful to have such wonderfully supportive colleagues at our home institutions.

In Ellis, though we cannot reveal their full names or the community's true identity, we must acknowledge Barb and Dave; Gary; Cindi; Alan; the great teachers, staff, and (past and present) students at the "Ellis Community School"; Terry; and all the people who allowed us to trample all over their lives.

Wendy Griswold, who was our guest while we lived in Iowa, helped us appreciate the lessons Iowa and Iowans have to teach us.

We are also immensely fortunate that Steve Schapiro, an amazing photographer, traveled to Ellis and helped tell this story through his great images.

Gayatri Patnaik, our editor at Beacon, had a passion for this project that has made all the difference. She was aided in her efforts "to get the book to the next level" by Allison Trzop and Joanna Green.

Amy Van Stee helped liberate us from our writing tics and overuse of several troublesome phrases.

Finally, we thank our friends and family, especially our children, Camille and Patrick John "P. J." Camille, who was just two years old when we lived in Iowa, was probably our best and most reliable fieldworker. Though our children share their parents' deep and abiding affection for Iowa, Camille (who is now nine years old) has wondered, with growing urgency, "When will the book be finished?"

Dearest Camille, thank you for your patience. Mommy and Daddy are, at last, done.

Notes

PREFACE

1. David Brooks, "One Nation, Slightly Divisible."

INTRODUCTION: THE HEARTLAND
AND THE RURAL YOUTH EXODUS

Calvin L. Beale, who died in September of 2008 at age eighty-five, was a senior demographer at the federal Agriculture Department, and his prodigious knowledge of rural America and influence on the research and policy in this area earned him the moniker "the Michael Jordan of rural research" (Barringer, 2008, http://www.nytimes.com/2008/09/03/us/03beale.html).

1. Richard Florida, *The Rise of the Creative Class.*
2. Richard Florida, "Creative Class War: How the GOP's Anti-Elitism Could Ruin America's Economy." http://creativeclass.com/rfcgdb/articles/Creative_Class_War.pdf.
3. United States Bureau of the Census, quoted in Matt Weiland and Sean Wilsey, eds., *State by State: A Panoramic Portrait of America,* 536.
4. In the nation, 2,052 nonmetropolitan counties occupy 97 percent of U.S. land area and are home to about one-fifth (almost 44.5 million people)

of the U.S. population. The Office of Management and Budget defines metro areas as (1) central counties with one or more urbanized areas, and (2) outlying counties that are economically tied to the core counties as measured by work commuting. Nonmetro counties are outside the boundaries of metro areas and are further subdivided into two types: micropolitan areas, which are centered on urban clusters of ten thousand or more persons, and all remaining "noncore" counties. Overall, in 2000, 17 percent of the national population lived in nonmetro counties, and 21 percent lived in rural areas. For the first time, a slight majority of rural people now live in metro areas ("Measuring Rurality?" USDA Briefing Room, www.ers.usda.gov/Briefing/Rurality/WhatIsRural/).

5. Willis Goudy, "Population Change in the Midwest Lags: Nonmetro Population Growth Lags Metro Increase."

6. There is a huge body of literature on the links between human-capital acquisition and geographic mobility and rural out-migration. For instance, see Thurston Domina, "What Clean Break? Education and Migration Patterns, 1989–2004," 378. Also see Daniel T. Lichter, Diane K. McLaughlin, and Gretchen T. Cornwell, "Migration and the Loss of Human Resources in Rural America," 235–56.

7. Thurston Domina, "Brain Drain and Brain Gain: Rising Educational Segregation in the United States, 1940–2000," 387.

8. The Higher Education Act of 1965 (or the HSA) was enacted on November 8, 1965, as part of President Lyndon Johnson's Great Society domestic agenda. The law was intended "to strengthen the educational resources of our colleges and universities and to provide financial assistance for students in postsecondary and higher education." It increased federal money given to universities, created scholarships, gave low-interest loans for students, and established a National Teachers Corps. The "financial assistance for students" is covered in Title IV of the HSA.

9. Domina, "Brain Drain," 387.

10. Ibid., 395.

11. Ibid.

12. Thurston Domina, "The Geography of Educational Segregation." www
.insidehighered.com/views/2007/01/19/domina.

13. Domina, "Brain Drain," 395.

14. Domina, "Geography."

15. In his 1920 masterpiece *Main Street,* Sinclair Lewis offers this description of the rural youth exodus: "With . . . small-town life . . . there are
hundreds of thousands . . . who are not content. The more intelligent
young people . . . flee to the cities . . . and . . . stay there, seldom returning even for holidays. The reason . . . is an unimaginatively standardized background, a sluggishness of speech and manners, a rigid ruling of
the spirit by the desire to appear respectable. It is contentment . . . the
contentment of the quiet dead, who are scornful of the living for their
restless walking" (257-58).

16. For an explanation of changes in agriculture, see Allan Barkema and
Mark Drabenstott, "Consolidation and Change in Heartland Agri-
culture." See also Richard Rathge and Paula Highman, "Population
Change in the Great Plains: A History of Prolonged Decline."

17. Monica Davey, "Vanishing Barns Signal a Changing Iowa," A1. www
.nytimes.com/2008/09/07/us/07iowa.html.

18. Kathryn M. Dudley, *Debt and Dispossession: Farm Loss in America's
Heartland* (Chicago and London: University of Chicago Press, 2000),
5. See also F. Larry Leistritz and Katherine Meyer, "Farm Crisis in the
Midwest: Trends and Implications."

19. Thomas Frank, *What's the Matter with Kansas? How Conservatives
Won the Heart of America,* 156.

20. Dudley, *Debt and Dispossession,* 5.

21. Economic Research Service, U.S. Department of Agriculture, *Understanding Rural America,* 5.

22. Dudley, *Debt and Dispossession,* 5.

23. William Julius Wilson, *The Truly Disadvantaged: The Inner City, the
Underclass, and Public Policy.*

24. It is difficult to offer a precise number for the loss of jobs in the manu-

facturing sector. Very often employers do not simply eliminate a position; they reduce the hours and benefits, making it easier to let workers go without having to cover the costs of terminating full-time workers.

25. Cited in Timothy Egan, "Pastoral Poverty: The Seeds of Decline." Data from the United States Department of Commerce. Also note that non-metropolitan counties have the highest poverty rates, and that of the 386 counties categorized as "persistent poverty" counties, 340 are non-metropolitan counties (USDA, "Rural Income").

26. Though rates of nonmarital childbearing in states such as Iowa still lag behind the national average, they are increasing.

27. See Gary W. Kendell, "Methamphetamine Abuse in Iowa: A Report to the Legislature." www.iowa.gov/odcp/docs/2007_Meth_Report_2-1-07.pdf. In yet another disturbing parallel to the inner city, the countryside's abundance of abandoned barns, easy access to fertilizer and ammonia (key ingredients for meth production), and growing supply of disconnected and disengaged young people offered a perfect storm of conditions for the growth of a rural drug trade; see Egan, "Pastoral Poverty."

28. This line is based on (but is not a direct quote from) Dale Maharidge's book *Denison, Iowa: Searching for the Soul of America through the Secrets of a Midwest Town,* 88. We have read similar lines about young people being Iowa's biggest export in Richard Longworth's *Caught in the Middle* and Stephen Bloom's *Postville.* The president of Saint Joseph's University, Father Timothy Lannon, SJ, a Harvard-educated Jesuit priest who was born, raised, and attended college in Iowa, said to Maria in 2002, "Iowa's greatest problem is that it exports all its young people." So we must credit all of them for this evocative line.

29. Florida, Richard, "The Rise of the Creative Class: Why Cities without Gays and Rock Bands Are Losing the Economic Development Race." www.washingtonmonthly.com/features/2001/0205.florida.html.

30. Florida, "Creative Class War." http://creativeclass.com/rfcgdb/articles/Creative_Class_War.pdf.

31. Egan, "Pastoral Poverty," B10.

32. Ibid.

33. For some of the most influential "creative cities" explanations of the concentration of educated, culturally sophisticated elites in metropolitan areas, see Heather Rogers, "Literary Amenities and Cultural Scenes: Assessing the Differential Impact of Quality and Spatial Concentration"; Terry N. Clark, "Urban Amenities: Lakes, Opera, and Juice Bars: Do They Drive Development?"; and Florida, *Rise of the Creative Class*.

34. Calvin Beale defines the Corn Belt and Great Plains this way: "If there is an idealized type of the agrarian and small-town image in America, it surely belongs to the Corn Belt and the Great Plains—the land of the Homestead Act, frugal, hard-working farmers, Garland's *Son of the Middle Border*, Rolvaag's *Giants in the Earth*, Lewis's *Main Street*, Inge's *Picnic*, Wilson's *Music Man*, and Grant Wood's *American Gothic*. A land of struggle—not always rewarded—and even occasional strife, but without the degrading legacy of slavery, sharecropping, grinding poverty, and soil depletion that has overlaid the rural South" (*A Taste of the Country: A Collection of Calvin Beale's Writings*, 65).

35. A recession in Iowa means manufacturing jobs most likely will get hammered. During the 1980s, when a national recession deepened into a farm crisis in Iowa and elsewhere in the Midwest, Iowa lost 43,100 factory jobs; 62 percent of all nonfarm positions were cut, state data show. And it was nearly as brutal two decades later, when the recession of 2001 wiped out nearly 32,000 factory jobs. Iowa has lost 2,400 factory jobs through September 2008, and more job losses are coming. Lennox Industries in Marshalltown, Whirlpool Corp. in Amana, and Rockwell Collins in Cedar Rapids announced an additional 1,000 cuts in October 2008. See Donnelle Eller, "How Will the Recession Hurt Iowa's Financial Sector?" www.desmoinesregister.com/article/20081116/BUSINESS/811160327/1029/BUSINESS.

36. William Schmidt, "Ups and Downs Aside, Iowa Has Middleness," A5.

37. In December 2002, when the Irish rock star Bono wanted to garner public support for his work on AIDS in Africa, he organized a bus tour of African performers to do shows throughout the Midwest, including Iowa. During the summer of that year, when we lived in Ellis, Bono also visited a Davenport, Iowa, truck stop to learn what "real" Americans think about the global AIDS crisis.

38. The notion of a "real" or more authentic America is an increasingly controversial claim that harkens back to the red- and blue-state culture wars. We use the term self-consciously to point out how the notion of an authentic America distracts us from the region's more serious concerns.

39. Osha Gray Davidson, *Broken Heartland: The Rise of America's Rural Ghetto*, 1.

40. Ibid.

41. Goudy, "Population Change."

42. Getting to Ellis, Iowa, from Philadelphia requires a flight into Chicago, then crop duster–style air travel to the tiny Waterloo Airport, then an hour's drive. When we traveled, the other air passengers were contractors working for John Deere, National Guard and Army reservists coming home from deployments and trainings, and, on one occasion, the body of an Iowan returning home for burial. The alternative route also took us to Chicago, then a connecting flight to Cedar Rapids, and a two-hour trip by car. When we moved to Ellis for the summer, we packed up our Nissan Altima (one of the only Japanese-made vehicles we ever saw in Liberty County) and settled into a rented, furnished two-bedroom house; our daughter, Camille, then two years old, christened our new residence the "summer house."

43. We interviewed people in fifteen states.

44. The research focused on two cohort sets of young people who had entered the high school as freshmen and would have graduated in 1990, 1991, or 1992 and 1995, 1996, and 1997. We assembled lists of the freshmen classes for these cohorts and, omitting foreign-exchange stu-

dents and students who started at Ellis but who graduated elsewhere, we distributed a short survey to almost 350 young adults. More than 80 percent completed the survey—some by telephone, some by mail—and from this group we completed in-depth interviews with 104 from February 2002 through March 2003. An extended discussion of the research design and detailed data from the survey and in-depth interviews are available at http://www.hollowingoutthemiddle.com.

45. According to the U.S. Census Bureau, 94.4 percent of the population in Iowa is white, making it the sixth whitest state (U.S. Census, 2009).

46. Richard Longworth, *Caught in the Middle*, 103.

47. Ibid.

48. Ibid.

49. Ibid.

50. Ibid.

51. Dean Krishna, "Try to Imagine the Iowa of My Dreams."

52. Liberty County is a made-up name for the county Ellis is in.

53. All of the names used in this book are pseudonyms.

54. One of the earliest documentations of the relationship between class and social reproduction in school appears in Robert and Helen Lynd's classic 1920s study *Middletown: A Study in Modern American Culture*. They write about the influence of a family's financial status on the educational outcomes of children, in many ways anticipating Annette Lareau's contemporary work on natural growth and concerted cultivation, *Unequal Childhoods: Class, Race, and Family Life*.

55. Garrison Keillor in his collection of essays titled *Leaving Home*, xiv.

56. In the piece "Palin's 'Pro-America Areas' Remark: Extended Version," the *Washington Post*'s Juliet Eilperin writes about the extended versions of Governor Palin's comments about the pro-America parts of the country and their contrast with Washington, D.C. (see http://voices .washingtonpost.com/44/2008/10/17/palin_clarifies_her_pro-americ .html). Like Barack Obama (see next note), Palin would later apologize for her comments. Palin explained she never intended to suggest that

specific parts of the country are less patriotic or less American. "If that's the way it has come across, I apologize," she told CNN's Drew Griffin. (From Lyndsey Layton, "Palin Apologizes for 'Real America' Comments," http://www.washingtonpost.com/wp-dyn/content/article/2008/ 10/21/AR2008102102449.html).

57. In April of 2008, presidential candidate Barack Obama told a crowd of supporters in San Francisco, "You go into some of these small towns in Pennsylvania, and like a lot of small towns in the Midwest, the jobs have been gone now for twenty-five years, and nothing's replaced them. And they fell through the Clinton administration, and the Bush administration, and each successive administration has said that somehow these communities are gonna regenerate, and they have not. And it's not surprising then they get bitter, they cling to guns or religion or antipathy to people who aren't like them or anti-immigrant sentiment or anti-trade sentiment as a way to explain their frustrations." The full quotation, which was spoken during a fundraiser in San Francisco, was first reported on the *Huffington Post* on April 11, 2008. In an October 15, 2008, *New York Times Magazine* cover story titled "Working for the Working-Class Vote," Senator Obama said that his greatest regret of the campaign, "my biggest boneheaded move," had been this comment. "How it was interpreted in the press was Obama talking to a bunch of wine-sipping San Francisco liberals with an anthropological view toward white working-class voters. And I was actually making the reverse point, clumsily, which is that these voters have a right to be frustrated because they've been ignored. And because Democrats haven't met them halfway on cultural issues, we've not been able to communicate to them effectively an economic agenda that would help broaden our coalition."

58. Layton, "Palin Apologizes."

59. See Thomas Frank, "Joe the Plumber and GOP Authenticity." http:// online.wsj.com/article/SB122463199532056477.html?mod=rss_The_ Tilting_Yard.

60. The Bristol Palin pregnancy and the announcement of her engagement, at age 17, brought into stark reality how rural teens might respond differently to early pregnancy. Though the details of Palin's situation are not widely known, the fact that the couple became engaged and presented themselves as a soon-to-be married couple matches the behaviors we saw in rural Iowa, where shotgun marriages have not gone out of style.

61. From an NPR interview with Richard Russo for *Morning Edition*, "Richard Russo's Small-Town America," October 1, 2007.

ONE: THE ACHIEVERS

1. In August Hollingshead's classic 1949 study, *Elmtown's Youth*, he argues that social class is the primary force determining young people's success in school. Mitchell Stevens, Elizabeth Armstrong, and Richard Arum write that "the idea that education might operate as a meritocratic corrective has defined the work of scholars and assorted activists for social change" ("Sieve, Incubator, Temple, Hub: Empirical and Theoretical Advances in the Sociology of Higher Education," 129). They go on to say that scholars such as Christopher Jencks and David Riesman (*The Academic Revolution*) remain far more skeptical and view education as a "social sieve" controlling access to privileged social positions. More recently, however, research finds that for young people in rural settings, educational goals are shaped by explicit and conscious commitments to rural life and place (see Caitlin Howley, "Purpose and Place: Schooling and Appalachian Residence," 63). In this sense, young people in rural settings are hindered or helped because of their ties to family and rural life (see also Glen Elder and Rand Conger, *Children of the Land: Adversity and Success in Rural America*; Cornelia and Jan Flora, *Rural Communities: Legacies and Change*; and Lynn Jamieson, "Migration, Place and Class: Youth in a Rural Area").

2. It certainly is worth mentioning that class factors into how young people get cultivated. Indeed, most recently, Annette Lareau, in her

influential book *Unequal Childhood,* coined the term "concerted cultivation" to describe how middle- and upper-middle-class parents manage their offspring's leisure activities to maximize their potential and achievement. What we are describing here is a variation of Lareau's ideas, which other scholars have noted, and we are extending that variation to a community as a whole that invests in young people. Indeed, what is striking about the Achievers from less affluent families is how they could deploy resources for one child and not another (see also Dalton Conley, *The Pecking Order: Which Siblings Succeed and Why*).

3. In her memoir, *Little Heathens: Hard Times and High Spirits on an Iowa Farm during the Great Depression,* Mildred Armstrong Kalish also speaks of the power of the small-town school. "Being a conscientious student who got good grades and would do anything to gain my teachers' favor, I was often granted special privileges and praised in front of my classmates. This was quite a contrast to my home environment where the adults were constantly critical of me. At home I couldn't do anything right; at school, I seemed to do everything right. So, school is where I wanted to be" (210).

4. Murray Milner, *Freaks, Geeks, and Cool Kids: American Teenagers and the Culture of Consumption.* We are indebted to Milner for this evocative parallel.

5. In the scholarship on education, the question of how students choose various curricula that lead to their distinctive outcomes is critical. For instance, Jencks et al. state in *Inequality: A Reassessment of the Effect of Family and Schooling in America:* "Some will choose curriculums that lead nowhere, because such curriculums involve less work in the short run. Some will eschew college, because they dislike the idea of spending 4 more years reading books. Some will avoid the high-status jobs because they are afraid of responsibility and even success. The fact that this happens does not prove that the student's educational opportunities were unequal; it proves that equal opportunity is not enough

to ensure equal results" (37). James Rosenbaum's case-study analysis of young people in a northeastern town he calls Grayton, *Making Inequality: The Hidden Curriculum of High School Tracking*, finds that guidance counselors mold the choices of their students "by the information they provide and withhold." He suggests, "Choice is the result of a complex interaction between the student and the school, and it must be measured in terms of real options the students are offered, the information they are given about the options, and the degree to which they are permitted to choose options the counselors consider ill-advised" (125). We find that there is definite structuring of choices but that the young people do claim agency over their fortunes.

6. See especially Pierre Bourdieu, *Distinction: A Social Critique of the Judgement of Taste.*

7. As in the previous chapter, it is important to note that we are not saying that there is a perfect class reproduction in Ellis. The sifting and sorting mechanism we depict here operates in very subtle ways that do favor those from privileged backgrounds—especially in the initial stages of the process. However, on occasion, a truly talented youth receives the nurturance and guidance of the wider community regardless of his or her background.

8. Tom Wolfe, *I Am Charlotte Simmons: A Novel.*

9. The rates of college participation have skyrocketed in the past thirty years, especially for young women. A National Center for Education Statistics report shows that for 18–24-year-olds "in 1974, young men participated in postsecondary education at a higher rate than young women (38 vs. 33 percent). Since 1974, both young men and young women have increased their rate of participation. However, the participation rate of young women outpaced that of young men, so that by 2003 participation patterns had reversed: 51 percent of young women had entered and/or completed postsecondary education, compared to 41 percent of young men" (Lisa Hudson, Sally Aquilino, and Gregory

Kienzl, "Postsecondary Participation Rates By Sex and Race/Ethnicity 1974–2003," 4).

10. For our young Iowans, exposure to the privileged world of college introduces them to new patterns of consumption and leisure but also to goals and expectations that mark them as authentic members of the elite. It is almost as if they become anthropologists, studying a new society. The Achievers will embrace what they see and go native; others will remain on the periphery and return home.

11. For years, journalistic accounts of hooking up and college drinking scenes have dominated the public's understanding of such worlds. In recent years, many scholars have provided insightful examinations of the lives of emerging adults on college campuses. See Elizabeth Armstrong and Laura Hamilton (*Exclusion: Class, Gender, and College Culture*, forthcoming) and also Kathleen Bogle (*Hooking Up: Sex, Dating, and Relationships on Campus*) and David Grazian (*On the Make: The Hustle of Urban Nightlife*). For an interesting discussion of how a group of lower-, working-, and upper-class young people manage their first year out of high school, also see Tim Clydesdale's *The First Year Out: Understanding American Teens after High School.*

12. In their retrospective accounts, the Achievers from more modest socioeconomic backgrounds describe college as an immersion experience in which they reshape their cultural capital to complement their aspirations for social mobility and mark themselves as authentic members of the status group to which they aspire to be a part. That said, there are moments when they can change course and abandon these goals. We will discuss the failed transformations in the Returner chapter, and, we hope, this will offers some insight into how higher education affects class identity and status.

TWO: THE STAYERS

1. H.G. Bissinger, *Friday Night Lights: A Town, a Team and a Dream,* 33.

2. Ibid.

3. According to an analysis of our survey of 275 young people who attended Ellis High School, we know that 43.3 percent currently reside in Ellis or a community within rural Liberty County (where Ellis is located); 26.9 percent reside outside of Iowa. Almost 30 percent currently live in Iowa but not in the rural area of Liberty County. The migration pattern out of Iowa within the Ellis sample mirrors the larger trends in the state. More detailed information is available at www.hollowing outthemiddle.com. Journalist Stephen Bloom and photographer Peter Feldstein chronicle the demographic shifts threatening rural Iowa in the collection of photographs and essays from their book *The Oxford Project*.

4. Social reproduction is the concept that, over time, groups of people, notably social classes, reproduce their social structure and patterns, reinforcing and passing on privilege and status.

5. This story is in line with findings from national data on high school aspirations and experience. For example, Robert Cobb, Walter McIntyre, and Phillip Pratt report that rural students are more likely than their urban and suburban counterparts to say that their guidance counselors and teachers do not think they ought to go to college ("Vocational and Educational Aspirations of High School Students: A Problem for Rural America").

6. There is no question that our account of the Stayers owes much to the influential studies of schooling and social reproduction. Among ethnographic studies of white working-class teenagers, Paul Willis's *Learning to Labor* and Jay MacLeod's *Ain't No Makin' It* are the ones we are most indebted to. MacLeod recently updated his classic with additional interviews of the Hallway Hangers and the Brothers as men in their forties, and the book now provides a sociological analysis by husband-wife sociologists Katherine McClelland and David Karen. The new work explores how delinquent, at-risk teens develop into fathers, husbands, and full-time workers who move away from crime, or do not. As we

find, social networks and the weaknesses of the postindustrial economy have limited what the Hallway Hangers and Brothers have managed to achieve. Our understanding is similar to McClelland and Karen's: "In this individualistic society, there is a relentless push to blame oneself and not the larger system" (448).

7. See Edward McCaul, "Rural Public School Dropouts: Findings from High School and Beyond," 19–24.

8. MacLeod, *Ain't No Makin' It*.

9. Cobb, McIntire, and Pratt, "Vocational and Educational Aspirations."

10. In an analysis of data gathered in the longitudinal survey "High School and Beyond (HSB)," Cobb, McIntire, and Pratt ("Vocational and Educational Aspirations") reported that, in comparison with urban young people, rural young people felt their parents were much more supportive of their taking full-time jobs, attending trade schools, or entering the military instead of attending college. These lower educational aspirations accompanied lower values for making a lot of money and higher values for simply making good incomes, having secure jobs, and maintaining friendships.

11. A third circumstance that influences the aspirations of rural students is the education level of their parents. Here, too, rural students suffer an early disadvantage. Seniors attending schools in metropolitan areas are 1.5 times more likely to have a parent with at least a bachelor's degree than nonmetropolitan students (Karen Pollard and William O'Hare, "Beyond High School: The Experience of Rural and Urban Youth in the 1980s"). This circumstance is unlikely to change, since the students who stay in rural America to become parents and raise families differ from those rural young people who leave. As a group, those who stay have the lowest educational aspirations of America's young people, and they tend to earn less than those who leave (Cobb, McIntire, and Pratt, "Vocational and Educational Aspirations").

12. In the growing body of work on emerging adulthood, many scholars have taken note of the class-segregated pathways in the transition to

adulthood. Frank Furstenberg et al. point out that while young elites delay their entry into marriage or establishment of an independent household, lower-class young people "fast-track" into childbearing but struggle to establish themselves financially and experience delays in establishing their own households ("Growing Up Is Harder to Do"). But among the young Iowans who are in the middle, we discover the accelerated transition to adulthood of the mid-twentieth century. This is made possible because of the enduring availability in rural areas of well-paid blue-collar jobs and a lower cost of living (namely, for housing) and a social context in which the more traditional patterns of marriage and family endure as normative.

13. McCaul, "Rural Public School Dropouts."

14. In *Caught in the Middle,* journalist Richard Longworth writes, "For a century, the Balls dominated the town. The company expanded into aluminum cans and then into satellites. Ball philanthropies made good things happen, including Ball State University, the town's leading employer. . . . Although never beautiful, Muncie was a solid, thriving place, exuding such an air of Midwestern normalcy that the sociologists Robert and Helen Lynd picked it for their classic study of an American 'Middletown'" (45–46).

15. This was particularly to the fore in the 2008 presidential primary campaigns in places such as Ohio, Pennsylvania, Indiana, and other states that have borne the brunt of the current economic slowdown. Success in the Democratic primaries in these states depends heavily on being able to court the "lunch-pail" Democrats.

16. Though Hillary Clinton and Barack Obama have similar positions on NAFTA, Clinton's has not been without controversy. Several commentators, including former Secretary of Labor Robert Reich, have said that she has executed a policy U-turn on NAFTA, going from being a proponent during the 1990s to being avowedly against it during the 2008 campaign. See, for instance, David Sirota, "Hillary Clinton's NAFTA U-Turn Says Something about Her—and Us"; and Robert Reich, "Hil-

lary and Barack, Afta Nafta," http://robertreich.blogspot.com/2008/02/
hillary-and-barack-afta-nafta.html.

17. See Reich, "Hillary and Barack."

18. In many cases, Iowa teens have now been replaced by migrant workers in these tasks.

19. In *Working and Growing Up in America*, Jeylan Mortimer studies how work prepares young people for adulthood by examining hours spent on the job and the intensity, duration, pattern, and quality of work. Mortimer makes the distinction between high-intensity and low-intensity but steady work, and she defines high-intensity work as when youth spend more than twenty hours per week in paid employment during high school. Mortimer demonstrates the significant consequences associated with the decision to work. She finds that young men and women with high-intensity jobs during high school are less likely to earn college degrees than are those who had steady but low-intensity work. Also, the youth who were in high-intensity jobs during high school were more likely than low-intensity workers to settle down, marry, and have children within seven years after high school.

20. When we conducted our study, Iowa's minimum wage was $5.15 an hour, the same amount as the federally mandated minimum wage, which has not changed since 1997. By 2006, twenty states and the District of Columbia had a minimum wage that exceeded the federal rate. Three of those states are Iowa's neighbors: Wisconsin, Minnesota, and Illinois. On January 25, 2007, Governor Chet Culver signed legislation increasing the Iowa minimum wage. Effective April 1, 2007, Iowa's minimum wage increased from $5.15 per hour to $6.20 per hour. On January 1, 2008, it increased to $7.25 per hour.

21. Many works have described the up-and-down circumstances of low-wage workers in the postindustrial economy, notably, Barbara Ehrenreich's *Nickel and Dimed: On (Not) Getting By in America*, David K. Shipler's *The Working Poor: Invisible in America*, Jason Deparle's *American Dream: Three Women, Ten Kids, and a Nation's Drive to End*

Welfare, and the more scholarly accounts, including Sharon Hays's *Flat Broke with Children: Women in the Age of Welfare Reform* and Kathryn Edin and Laura Lein's *Making Ends Meet: How Single Mothers Survive Welfare and Low-Wage Work.*

22. Researchers find that when faced with pregnancy, couples in metropolitan settings opt for cohabitation. In rural settings, these same couples are far more likely to enter marriage and marry much younger. See Snyder, Brown, and Condo's article "Residential Differences in Family Formation: The Significance of Cohabitation."

23. In her controversial book, *Unhooked: How Young Women Pursue Sex, Delay Love and Lose at Both,* Laura Stepp, a Pulitzer Prize–winning *Washington Post* reporter, writes about how smart, ambitious young women do emotional damage to themselves by getting physical—from making out to having sex—with men they are not dating or may have met for the first time. Her critique of the hook-up culture offers an interesting counterpoint to the fact that working-class young women and many of the Stayers in Iowa who don't pursue higher education follow the traditional dating patterns that Stepp mourns the loss of in contemporary youth culture.

24. The social norms that pressure young people to marry when there is a pregnancy still exist here in Ellis. But increasingly, as Kathryn Edin and Maria Kefalas find among the low-income, urban, single mothers they study, shotgun weddings have been replaced by shotgun cohabitations (*Promises I Can Keep: Why Poor Women Put Motherhood over Marriage*). Many of the single mothers we spoke to said they entered marriage because of pregnancy. However, it is worth noting that this behavior is breaking down, and the rate of nonmarital childbearing is on the rise. One in four births to Iowa women is to an unmarried mother. The markers of being a fast-starter, for example, age at first marriage, vary widely by geography. In Iowa, the median age at first marriage is twenty-four for women and twenty-five for men, which is just a year below the national average of twenty-five for women and twenty-six

for men. People in rural states, particularly southern ones, have more marriages, and these usually happen earlier in life. In Arkansas, for instance, more than a third of women ages eighteen to twenty-four are married, whereas in Massachusetts only about 13 percent are. Iowa occupies a middle ground, with just more than one-fifth of the young women in this age group being married. In our Ellis sample, the average age of women marrying for the first time was approximately twenty-three. For more information on these trends, see Susan Jekielek and Brett Brown, "The Transition to Adulthood: Characteristics of Young Adults Ages 18 to 24 in America."

25. See Snyder, Brown, and Condo, "Residential Differences."

26. A wonderfully succinct summary of the difference between rural and urban poverty from Alex Kotlowitz's *Frontline* PBS documentary called "Let's Get Married: Are the Conservatives Right?"

27. "Even after two decades of decreasing rates, suicide remains the third leading cause of death among youth between the ages of 10 and 24.2. Moreover, the declines are not evenly distributed. In fifteen states, youth suicide rates remain as high as or even higher than the twenty-year peak of 9.36 suicides per 100,000 [in this age group]. Three western and mountain states consistently have higher suicide rates than the rest of the country, and all of the states with the highest suicide rates have many counties that would meet most definitions of 'rural'—that is, with very low population density and residents living in relatively small communities, separated by vast landscapes" (Rural Youth Suicide Prevention Workgroup, "Preventing Youth Suicide in Rural America: Recommendations for States," 4).

28. As a state, Iowa has low rates for teen pregnancy; it is ranked forty-sixth out of the fifty states. This is probably a result of the effectiveness of the state's educational system. Graduating from high school is a natural retardant to early childbearing. Nationally, rural areas have teen pregnancy rates that are somewhat lower than urban areas and higher than suburban areas. Little is known about rural adolescent sexual be-

havior; what is known is that (1) there is younger age at first sexual experience, (2) there is earlier childbearing, (3) it is more common to marry after a nonmarital pregnancy, so there is a closer link between marriage and childbearing, and (4) there is a trend toward earlier marriage. See Anastasia R. Snyder, "Teen Pregnancy, Rural Poverty, and Youth Well-Being Outcomes."

29. Iowa has the fourth-highest rate of alcohol consumption of any state in the Union.

30. See Katherine Newman et al. in *Rampage* for a fascinating discussion of why school shootings are more likely to occur in rural communities. Indeed, Newman notes that the successful supervision of young people's minor acts of deviance lulls residents into the self-deceiving perception that nothing else more serious takes place.

31. Timothy Egan, "Pastoral Poverty: The Seeds of Decline," A1.

32. Ibid.

33. Tweaking occurs when a meth addict has used large amounts of meth, probably has not slept in several days, and is irritable and paranoid. An addict who is tweaking can appear normal but is likely to be unpredictable and has the potential to become dangerous.

34. After five years of living among and learning from crack dealers in East Harlem, anthropologist Philippe Bourgois agrees. In *In Search of Respect: Selling Crack in El Barrio*, Bourgois argues that "drugs provide an illusory escape from oppression. Instantaneously," he writes, "the user is transformed from an unemployed, depressed high school dropout, despised by the world—and secretly convinced that his failure is due to his own inherent stupidity and disorganization."

THREE: THE SEEKERS

1. Even though school administrators may try to restrict access, recruiters politely and insistently request that schools provide them with yearbooks, transcripts, and office space. When the Ellis principal once declined to comply, he was strongly pressured by the recruiters to provide

the requested materials. Nationally, the issue of getting information about young people has made parents and school officials uncomfortable. In 2004, the Pentagon contracted with a marketing firm, BeNow, Inc., to collect and consolidate data about high school students as young as sixteen, as well as college students. The data include ethnicity, e-mail addresses, GPAs, subjects studied, and Social Security numbers from commercial sources and state's driver's license records.

2. For a marvelous account of the admissions process at elite private colleges, see Mitchell Stevens's award-winning book, *Creating a Class: College Admissions and the Education of Elites*.

3. National Priorities Project, *Military Recruiting 2006*. The report shows how the recruiting and advertising budget includes Department of Defense spending on operating the recruitment stations and advertising. The budget rose to $1.5 billion in 2005 and surpassed $1.8 billion in the 2007 fiscal year. However, that amount does not include the pay and benefits of twenty-two thousand military recruiters and recruiting-related spending such as enlistment bonuses used to entice new recruits.

4. Steve Coll, "Military Conflict," 21.

5. Tom Vanden Brook, "Bonuses Boost Reservist's Recruitment," 6.

6. See National Priorities Project, *Military Recruiting 2006*. See especially the top hundred counties by recruits per thousand youth.

7. This ranking is based on data analyzed by the National Priorities Project, in which states were ranked based on numbers of active-duty military recruits per thousand youth for the fiscal year 2006. Although Iowa, with 3.5 active recruits per thousand, is slightly below the national average of 3.8, the state sends the largest proportion of "high-quality" recruits into the armed forces. And in 2006, Iowa's Crawford and Lee counties ranked among the nation's top one hundred counties for military recruits.

8. See Maria's discussion of the local-level construction of the nation in her ethnographic account of a white, working- and lower-middle-

class Chicago neighborhood renamed Beltway in the book *Working-Class Heroes: Protecting Home, Community, and Nation in a Chicago Neighborhood.*

9. See Beth Bailey's important article "The Army in the Marketplace" for a historical perspective on the all-volunteer force and the original efforts for recruitment.

10. In 2008, the meat-processing firm Agriprocessors, located in Postville, Iowa, the nation's largest kosher meatpacker, faced criminal charges for more than nine thousand child labor violations. According to a September 9, 2008, article by Julia Preston in the *New York Times:*

> The Iowa attorney general on Tuesday brought an array of criminal charges for child-labor violations against the owners and top managers of a meatpacking plant where nearly four hundred workers were detained in a May immigration raid. . . . In all, 9,311 criminal misdemeanor charges involving thirty-two underage workers were filed against the company, Agriprocessors Inc., and its owner, Aaron Rubashkin, and his son Sholom, who was the top manager of the packing plant in Postville, Iowa. The complaint charges that the plant employed workers under the legal age of eighteen, including seven who were under sixteen, from Sept. 9, 2007, to May 12. Some workers, including some younger than sixteen, worked on machinery prohibited for employees under eighteen, including "conveyor belts, meat grinders, circular saws, power washers and power shears," said an affidavit filed with the complaint ("Meatpacker Faces Charges of Violating Child Labor Laws," A16).

11. Evan Wright, *Generation Kill: Devil Dogs, Iceman, Captain America, and the New Face of American War.*

12. Helen Benedict, *The Lonely Soldier: The Private War of Women Serving in Iraq.*

13. In October 2006, the late military sociologist Charles Moskos corre-

sponded with Maria and passed on to her a rough draft of an unpub-
lished op-ed piece titled "How Can We Save the All-Volunteer Army?"
In it, he calls for a return to the draft or, failing that, a recruitment
campaign that targets college graduates:

> It is no secret that Army recruitment is in deep trouble. In par-
> ticular, recruitment for reserve components is on the brink of
> disaster. This has led some (including this writer) to call for
> mandatory national service. But the political reality is that there
> is little chance of any form of conscription. Indeed, in the last
> election, both President Bush and Senator Kerry were united in
> their opposition to bring back the draft. So what can be done to
> fix the personnel problems of the all-volunteer force? The only
> way to alleviate recruitment shortfalls is to introduce an enlist-
> ment option targeted at college graduates. Two-thirds of Amer-
> ican high school graduates now go directly on to some form of
> higher education. Of these, about half—1.2 million annually—
> will graduate with a bachelor's degree. Yet military recruitment
> of college graduates at the enlisted level is minuscule.

FOUR: THE RETURNERS

1. Jim Tankersley and Christi Parsons, "Immigration Roils Small-Town
   America."
2. Alex Kotlowitz, "Our Town." In fact, the Carpentersville example is
   of particular interest because some of the people who have become so
   vehemently opposed to immigration in the town had served on the Hispanic Committee, a group that was formed in 1999 to "help acculturate
   and celebrate the new arrivals." The Hispanic Committee sponsored
   voter registration and a Celebration Latina but disbanded a little more
   than a year after it was formed, notably after changing the name of the
   fete to Community Pride Day.
3. Charles M. Tolbert, Michael D. Irwin, Thomas A. Lyson, and Albert R.

Nucci, "Civic Community in Small-Town America: How Civic Welfare Is Influenced by Local Capitalism and Civic Engagement."

4. The push to bring three hundred thousand people to Iowa included attracting High-Flyers and skilled immigrants, the latter campaign being the other major Vilsack initiative to combat the brain drain.

5. Generation Iowa Commission, Status Report.

6. The GIC 2008 report trumpets the fact that Iowa's wages are 20 percent below the national average, and this affects where members of the Next Generation will seek work after finishing their education. The report goes on to say that "the Next Generation is pragmatic and economically driven. They will only stay in Iowa if they can find a great job with a competitive salary and a good chance for professional growth" (16).

7. Google's $600-million Iowa data center project is under construction on a fifty-five-acre site at the Council Bluffs Industrial Foundation's new business park and is expected to open in spring 2009. The two-building project includes the purchase of an abandoned industrial building, which will be retrofitted to suit Google's needs.

8. Bridget Botelho, "Google's Iowa Data Center Smart Move, Experts Say."

9. John Foley, "Why Google and Microsoft Are Building Data Centers in Iowa."

10. Generation Iowa Commission, Report Recommendations.

11. In every state, the proportion of blacks in prison exceeds, sometimes by a considerable amount, their proportion in the general population. Yet "in Minnesota and Iowa, blacks constitute a share of the prison population that is twelve times greater than their share of the state population." Moreover, nationwide, a black person is 8.2 times more likely to be in prison than a white person. Among individual states, there are even more extraordinary racial disparities in incarceration rates. In seven states—Connecticut, Illinois, Iowa, Minnesota, New Jersey, Pennsylvania, and Wisconsin—blacks are incarcerated at more than 13 times the rate of whites (Human Rights Watch, "Incarceration and Race").

12. The call for the constitutional ban has not gained traction, and, at the time of this writing, Iowa remained a long shot for the recognition of gay-partner unions. It is worth noting that the consensus opinion among many Republicans was to oppose gay marriage and leave it up to the states to create policies for gay partnerships.

13. 365gay Newscenter Staff, "60 Percent in Iowa Support Gay Couple Rights."

14. See Osgood et al. ("Six Paths to Adulthood") about the various distinctive trajectories into adulthood. The Iowans who remain in the state follow a pattern that Osgood et al. categorize as the "fast-starters" and "parents without careers." For an overview of the transition to adulthood, see Richard Settersten, Frank Furstenberg Jr., and Ruben Rumbaut, *On the Frontier of Adulthood: Theory, Research and Public Policy.*

15. The Chops logo is a snarling hog, and there has been a great deal of criticism of the name and logo since they were unveiled in the summer of 2008.

16. The actual proportion of counties that have a medically underserved area is 58 percent, according to the U.S. Department of Health and Human Services, Health Resources and Services Administration. Fifty-six of the state's ninety-seven counties have at least one underserved area, and many counties have several.

17. Omaha, a city of about four hundred thousand people, recorded an average of twenty-nine homicides a year for the period 2000–2005, corresponding to a rate of a little more than seven per one hundred thousand. Although this is not a high rate, it contrasts markedly with Ellis, which has not had a recorded homicide in more than three decades.

18. From the Web site "What Is Cool Cities?" (www.coolcities.com/whatscool/background/), which is maintained by the Michigan Department of Labor and Economic Growth.

19. Sue Burzynski-Bullard, "State's College Graduates Still Make Run for Border: Cool Cities Don't Impress Students Who Mostly Want Jobs."

20. Ibid.

21. Associated Press, "N.O. Lawmaker Wants Housing Aid for College Graduates."

22. Burzynski-Bullard, "State's College Graduates."

23. Minnesota Department of Employment and Economic Development "Bioscience Zone," www.positivelyminnesota.com/biozone/biosciZone .htm.

24. Laura French, "Minnesota Is a Natural for Bioscience."

25. See the map in Calvin Beale, "Non-metro County Population Change 2000–05: Half Grew, Half Declined."

CONCLUSION

1. For instance, the Ellis-Stearns Iowa Test of Educational Development scores for math and reading taken in eleventh grade are consistently above the state average, with the math scores 17 percent above state averages in 2007.

2. See Wendell Pritchett's fascinating biography of the first black cabinet secretary (Department of Housing and Urban Development), *Robert Clifton Weaver and the American City: The Life and Times of an Urban Reformer*. Pritchett asserts that Weaver shaped the development of American racial and urban policy. He finds that Weaver made his way into the cabinet not solely as an urban reformer but also, although he chafed at this description of his responsibility, as the "Negro" adviser.

3. In a December 2001 piece for the *Atlantic*, "One Nation, Slightly Divisible," journalist David Brooks, who regularly engages in a form of journalism strongly influenced by sociology, describes his methods for comparing Blue and Red America this way: "I went to [Pennsylvania's] Franklin County because I wanted to get a sense of how deep the divide really is, to see how people there live, and to gauge how different their lives are from those in my part of America. I spoke with ministers, journalists, teachers, community leaders, and pretty much anyone I ran

across. I consulted with pollsters, demographers, and market-research firms." We have assumed that he did not run into any of the people we have just mentioned.

4. In "The Rise and Fall of Social Problems: A Public Arenas Model," Stephen Hilgartner and Charles Bosk point out that raising awareness of particular social concerns is a crucial, and maybe the most challenging, step in generating interest around a social issue. Certainly, the creation of HUD grew out of the racial unrest in American cities, but the crisis in rural America has been far quieter and less obvious to the rest of the nation, and no comparable bureaucracy has been created in response.

5. Karl Stauber, "Why Invest in Rural America—and How? A Critical Public Policy Question for the Twenty-first Century," 27.

6. Based on e-mail correspondence on December 1, 2008.

7. Richard Florida, *Rise of the Creative Class*. See also David A. McGranahan and Timothy R. Wojan, "Recasting the Creative Class to Examine Growth Processes in Rural and Urban Counties"; and Timothy R. Wojan and David A. McGranahan, "Ambient Returns: Creative Capital's Contribution to Local Manufacturing Competitiveness."

8. David A. McGranahan and Timothy R. Wojan, "The Creative Class: A Key to Rural Growth," 17.

9. The Maharishi International University is in Fairfield in Jefferson County, and it is a magnet for people interested in transcendental meditation. Many of the people who have moved to Jefferson County have done so because of the university, and a large number of these people are in creative-class occupations.

10. McGranahan and Wojan, "Recasting the Creative Class."

11. Robert E. Land, Andrea Sarzynski, and Mark Muro, "Mountain Megas: America's Newest Metropolitan Places and a Partnership to Help Them Prosper."

12. Donnelle Eller, "How Will Economy Affect Iowa's Financial Sector?"

13. Richard Longworth, *Caught in the Middle: America's Heartland in the Age of Globalism.*

14. Ibid., 98.

15. It should be noted that Longworth does not focus exclusively on small towns. In fact, he spends as much time chronicling the decline of the likes of Dayton, Detroit, and Muncie as he does on places like Ellis.

16. Timothy Collins, "'Tough Love' for Tough Times in the Midwest."

17. Ibid.

18. Maria Surma Manka, "Midwest Monday: Iowa Guv Talks Solar Power."

19. New Iowans Pilot Project, "Recruiting New Iowans into Model Communities."

20. Ibid.

21. Iowa Center for Immigrant Leadership and Integration, Mission Statement, www.bcs.uni.edu/ICILI/mission.htm.

22. Ibid.

23. Mark Grey, Nora Rodriguez, and Andrew Conrad, "Immigrant and Refugee Small Business Development in Northeast Iowa."

24. August Gribben, "Iowa Makes English Official; Advocates Believe That English Is the Glue That Unites Social Groups and Nurtures Civic Responsibility."

25. Indeed, it is probably fair to point out that Vilsack's attempt to corral the macroeconomic forces epitomized by agribusiness was doomed to failure from the outset. Vilsack wanted to lure skilled workers, but meat processors and similar labor-intensive rural employers demanded abundant sources of cheap, unskilled labor. The mismatch was apparent, although the consequences—the depression of entry-level wages, the lengthening of work days, curtailing of benefits, and, above all, the replacement of natives with imported labor—were probably unanticipated.

26. Christopher Conte, "Strangers on the Prairie."

27. Donald D. Stull, Michael J. Broadway, and David Griffith, *Any Way You Cut It: Meat Processing and Small-Town America.*

28. Ibid.

29. See Mark Grey, "Pork, Poultry, and Newcomers in Storm Lake, Iowa."

See also David Griffith, "*Hay Trabajo:* Poultry Processing, Rural Industrialization, and the Latinization of Low-Wage Labor."

30. Thomas Frank, "Captives of the Meatpacking Archipelago."

31. William Petroski, "Taxpayers' Costs Top $5 Million for May Raid at Postville."

32. The city was named an All-American City in 2007 for its various civic initiatives involving immigrants, youth, and economic development.

33. See www.htccommunity.org/?PHPSESSID=2b802ca85bafb8cae511b8 0eocebee56.

34. Ibid.

35. John Ritter, "Towns Offer Free Land to Newcomers."

36. Marti Attoun, "Where the Land Is Free."

37. Sonya Salamon's wonderful book *Newcomers to Old Towns* chronicles the experiences of six "post-agrarian" towns in Illinois as they attract newcomers fleeing metropolitan areas for a place in the country. Salamon skillfully depicts what she calls rural suburbanization, which is possible because of the proximity to larger metropolitan areas. In contrast, the towns giving away land are not in any danger of becoming suburbs of anywhere.

38. Calvin Beale and Kenneth Johnson, "The Identification of Recreational Counties in Nonmetropolitan Areas of the USA."

39. Ritter, "Towns Offer Free Land."

40. Ibid.

41. The New Homestead Act 2007, sponsored by Senator Byron Dorgan (D-ND) and cosponsored by Senator Chuck Hagel (R-NE), was introduced to the U.S. Senate for the third time on April 12, 2007. The bill was read twice and referred to the Committee on Finance, where it currently resides.

42. See Deborah Popper and Frank Popper, "Great Plains: From Dust to Dust" and "The Buffalo Commons: Then and Now."

43. Popper and Popper, "Great Plains," 18.

44. Florence Williams, "Frank and Deborah Popper's 'Buffalo Commons' Is Creeping toward Reality."

45. Ibid.

46. Popper and Popper, "The Buffalo Commons," 19.

47. Williams, "Frank and Deborah."

48. Ibid.

49. In "Vanishing Barns Signal a Changing Iowa," Monica Davey writes that "the tale of the disappearing barn, a building whose purpose shifted, then faded away, tells a bigger story too, of how farming itself, a staple in this state then and now, has changed markedly."

50. Research on career academies has shown that youth who participate in the program, especially young men, have significantly higher earnings over a period of years, more job stability, and a greater likelihood to live independently than peers who are not in career academies. See James J. Kemple and Cynthia J. Willner, "Career Academies: Long-term Impacts on Labor Market Outcomes, Educational Attainment, and Transitions to Adulthood." Our call for better links among high schools, community colleges, and employers echoes the views of Northwestern University's James Rosenbaum (*Beyond College for All: Career Paths for the Forgotten Half*) and, more recently, Charles Murray (*Real Education: Four Simple Truths for Bringing America's Schools Back to Reality*). We are all troubled by how investing so heavily in educational programs geared to the goal of students earning bachelor's degrees fails to serve the interests of large numbers of students.

51. News Release, Kansas Department of Commerce, May 21, 2008. www .kansascommerce.com/Services/News/NewsReleaseDetail.aspx? postID=546.

52. Ibid.

53. One of the more contentious issues during the 2008 presidential election was energy policy. Republicans and Democrats agreed on the need to become energy independent, but they differed on the methods to

achieve this goal. For the Democrats, the path to energy independence included the creation of five million jobs in the green energy sector, many of them in wind and solar provision. See http://my.barackobama .com/page/content/newenergy for more details.

54. Georgeanne Artz, "Rural Area Brain Drain: Is It a Reality?"

55. See Kenneth M. Johnson and Daniel T. Lichter, "Natural Increase: A New Source of Population Growth in Emerging Hispanic Destinations." Also Leif Jensen, "New Immigrant Settlements in Rural America: Problems, Prospects and Policies."

56. Grey, Rodriguez, and Conrad, "Immigrant and Refugee," 6.

57. Domenico Parisi and Daniel T. Lichter, "Hispanic Segregation in America's New Rural Boomtowns."

58. Ibid.

59. Osha Gray Davidson, *Broken Heartland: The Rise of America's Rural Ghetto.*

60. Thomas Frank, "Captives."

61. For instance, a *New York Times* report on December 13, 2008, detailed the ultimately successful fifteen-year fight by workers at the Smithfield Packing Slaughterhouse in Tar Heel, North Carolina, to organize a local of the United Food and Commercial Workers' Union. See Steven Greenhouse, "After 15 Years, North Carolina Plant Unionizes."

62. Parisi and Lichter, "Natural Increase."

63. Doug Massey and Nancy Denton, *American Apartheid: Segregation and the Making of the American Underclass.*

64. It is interesting that one of the few state-produced campaigns—IOWA *life*|Changing—features a testimonial from Zoraida DeFreitas, who grew up in Caracas, Venezuela. Zoraida works in bioscience, and she talks about how much she enjoys life in Iowa with her husband. She could be a poster child for an immigrant who has acclimatized to the region and who adds considerably to the community. However, Zoraida has a fair complexion and long blonde hair, and she resembles the

original Swedish homesteaders more than she does the greater Hispanic diaspora of which she is a part.

65. In 2006, Hazleton mayor Lou Barletta penned an open letter to immigrants in Hazleton that simply said, "You are no longer welcome." The city passed a series of ordinances that prohibited local businesses from hiring undocumented workers. This backlash in Hazleton had been prompted by two shooting incidents and an illegal-drug seizure in the town, all involving undocumented immigrants, and Barletta received national attention for his attempt to craft what amounted to a local immigration policy.

66. Michael Pollan, "Farmer in Chief," *New York Times*, October 12, 2008, MM62.

67. Ibid.

68. Thomas Frank, personal communication, February 22, 2009.

References

365gay Newscenter Staff. "60 Percent in Iowa Support Gay Couple Rights." November 26, 2008.

Albrecht, Don E., and Carol M. Albrecht. "Metro/Nonmetro Residence, Nonmarital Conception and Conception Outcomes." *Rural Sociology* 69, no. 3 (2004): 430–52.

Armstrong, Elizabeth A., and Laura Hamilton. *Exclusion: Class, Gender, and College Culture.* Cambridge, MA: Harvard University Press, forthcoming 2010.

Artz, Georgeanne. "Rural Area Brain Drain: Is It a Reality?" *Choices*, 4th quarter, 2003.

Associated Press. "N.O. Lawmaker Wants Housing Aid for College Graduates." *New Orleans City Business*, June 2, 2008.

Attoun, Marti. "Where the Land Is Free." *American Profile.com* (2006), www.americanprofile.com/article/5285.html.

Bai, Matt. "Working for the Working-Class Vote." *New York Times Magazine*, October 19, 2008.

Bailey, Beth. "The Army in the Marketplace." *Journal of American History* 94, no. 1 (2007): 47–74.

Barkema, Allan, and Mark Drabenstott. "Consolidation and Change in Heartland Agriculture." In *Economic Forces Shaping the Rural Heartland*, ed. Mark Drabenstott. Kansas City: Federal Reserve Bank of Kansas City, 1996.

Barringer, Felicity. "Calvin L. Beale, Demographer with a Feel for Rural America, Dies at 85." *New York Times*, September 2, 2008.

Beale, Calvin. "Non-metro County Population Change 2000–05: Half Grew, Half Declined." *Amber Waves* 4, no. 3 (2006): 57.

_____. *A Taste of the Country: A Collection of Calvin Beale's Writings.* Edited by Peter Morrison. University Park: Pennsylvania State University Press, 1990.

Beale, Calvin, and Kenneth Johnson. "The Identification of Recreational Counties in Nonmetropolitan Areas of the USA." *Population Research and Policy Review* 17, no. 1 (1998): 37–53.

Benedict, Helen. *The Lonely Soldier: The Private War of Women Serving in Iraq.* Boston: Beacon Press, 2009.

Bissinger, H. G. *Friday Night Lights: A Town, a Team, and a Dream.* New York: DaCapo Books, 1990.

Bloom, Stephen. *Postville: A Clash of Cultures in Heartland America.* Orlando, FL: Harcourt, 2000.

Bloom, Stephen, and Peter Feldstein. *The Oxford Project.* New York: Welcome Books, 2008.

Bogle, Kathleen. *Hooking Up: Sex, Dating, and Relationships on Campus.* New York: NYU Press, 2008.

Botelho, Bridget. "Google's Iowa Data Center Smart Move, Experts Say." *Data Center News*, June 26, 2007.

Bourdieu, Pierre. *Distinction: A Social Critique of the Judgement of Taste.* Cambridge, MA: Harvard University Press, 1984.

Bourgois, Philippe. *In Search of Respect: Selling Crack in El Barrio.* New York: Cambridge University Press, 2002.

Brooks, David. "One Nation, Slightly Divisible." *Atlantic*, December 2001.

Burzynski-Bullard, Sue. "State's College Graduates Still Make Run for Border: Cool Cities Don't Impress Students Who Mostly Want Jobs." *Detroit News*, May 15, 2008.

Clark, Terry Nichols. "Urban Amenities: Lakes, Opera, and Juice Bars: Do

They Drive Development?" In *The City as an Entertainment Machine,* ed. Terry Nichols Clark. Oxford, England: JAI/Elsevier, 2003.

Clydesdale, Tim. *The First Year Out: Understanding American Teens after High School.* Chicago: University of Chicago Press, 2007.

Cobb, Robert A., Walter G. McIntire, and Phillip A. Pratt. "Vocational and Educational Aspirations of High School Students: A Problem for Rural America." *Research in Rural Education* 6, no. 2 (1989): 11–16.

Coll, Steve. "Military Conflict." *New Yorker,* April 14, 2008.

Collins, Timothy. "'Tough Love' for Tough Times in the Midwest." *Daily Yonder* (2008), available at www.dailyyonder.com/tough-love-tough-times-midwest.

Conley, Dalton. *The Pecking Order: Which Siblings Succeed and Why.* New York: Pantheon, 2004.

Conte, Christopher. "Strangers on the Prairie." *Governing,* January 2002.

Davey, Monica. "Vanishing Barns Signal a Changing Iowa." *New York Times,* September 7, 2008, A1.

Davidson, Osha Gray. *Broken Heartland: The Rise of America's Rural Ghetto.* Iowa City: University of Iowa Press, 1996.

Deparle, Jason. *American Dream: Three Women, Ten Kids, and a Nation's Drive to End Welfare.* New York: Viking, 2004.

Domina, Thurston. "Brain Drain and Brain Gain: Rising Educational Segregation in the United States, 1940–2000." *City and Community* 5, no. 4 (2006): 387–407.

———. "The Geography of Educational Segregation." *Inside Higher Education* January 19 (2007), available at www.insidehighered.com/views/2007/01/19/domina.

———. "What Clean Break? Education and Migration Patterns, 1989–2004." *Rural Sociology* 71, no. 3 (2006): 373–98.

Dudley, Kathryn M. *Debt and Dispossession: Farm Loss in America's Heartland.* Chicago and London: University of Chicago Press, 2000.

Edin, Kathryn, and Maria J. Kefalas. *Promises I Can Keep: Why Poor*

Women Put Motherhood over Marriage. Berkeley: University of California Press, 2005.

Edin, Kathryn, and Laura Lein. *Making Ends Meet: How Single Mothers Survive Welfare and Low Wage Work.* New York: Russell Sage Foundation, 1997.

Egan, Timothy. "Pastoral Poverty: The Seeds of Decline." *New York Times,* December 8, 2002, B1, B10.

Ehrenreich, Barbara. *Nickel and Dimed: On (Not) Getting By in America.* New York: Holt, 2002.

Eilperin, Juliet. "Palin's 'Pro-America Areas' Remark: Extended Version." *Washington Post Online,* October 17, 2008.

Elder, Glen H. Jr., and Rand D. Conger. *Children of the Land: Adversity and Success in Rural America.* Chicago: University of Chicago Press, 2000.

Eller, Donnelle. "How Will Economy Affect Iowa's Financial Sector?" *Des Moines Register,* November 16, 2008.

Flora, Cornelia B., and Jan A. Flora. *Rural Communities: Legacies and Change.* 2nd ed. Boulder, CO: Westview Press, 2004.

Florida, Richard. "Creative Class War: How the GOP's Anti-Elitism Could Ruin America's Economy." *Washington Monthly,* January/February 2004, 30–37.

_____. *The Rise of the Creative Class.* New York: Basic Books, 2002.

_____. "The Rise of the Creative Class: Why Cities without Gays and Rock Bands Are Losing the Economic Development Race." *Washington Monthly,* May 2002, 15–26.

Foley, John. "Why Google and Microsoft Are Building Data Centers in Iowa." *Information Week,* August 4, 2008, 10.

Frank, Thomas. "Captives of the Meatpacking Archipelago." *Wall Street Journal,* August 6, 2008, A13.

_____. "Joe the Plumber and GOP Authenticity." *Wall Street Journal,* October 22, 2008, A15.

_____. *What's the Matter with Kansas? How Conservatives Won the Heart of America*. New York: Metropolitan Books, 2005.

French, Laura. "Minnesota Is a Natural for Bioscience." *Minnesota Star Tribune*, March 5, 2007.

Furstenberg, Frank F. Jr., Sheela Kennedy, Vonnie C. McLloyd, Rubén G. Rumbaut, and Richard A. Settersten Jr. "Growing Up Is Harder to Do." *Contexts* 3, no. 3 (2004): 33–41.

Generation Iowa Commission. *Report Recommendations*. Des Moines, IA, 2007, www.iowalifechanging.com/generation/downloads/gen-iowa-report-2007-RECCOMMENDATIONSONLY.pdf.

_____. *Status Report*. Des Moines, IA, December 2008. www.iowalife changing.com/generation/downloads/gen-iowa-report-2008-final .pdf.

Goudy, Willis. "Population Change in the Midwest Lags: Nonmetro Population Growth Lags Metro Increase." *Rural America* 17, no. 2 (2002): 21–29.

Grazian, David. *On the Make: The Hustle of Urban Nightlife*. Chicago: University of Chicago Press, 2007.

Greenhouse, Steven. "After 15 Years, North Carolina Plant Unionizes." *New York Times*, December 12, 2008, A1.

Grey, Mark. "Pork, Poultry and Newcomers in Storm Lake, Iowa." In *Any Way You Cut It*, eds. Donald D. Stull, Michael J. Broadway, and David Griffith. Lawrence: University Press of Kansas, 1995.

_____, Nora Rodriguez, and Andrew Conrad. "Immigrant and Refugee Small Business Development in Northeast Iowa." New Iowans Program, University of Northern Iowa, 2004.

Gribben, August. "Iowa Makes English Official; Advocates Believe That English Is the Glue That Unites Social Groups and Nurtures Civic Responsibility." *Insight on the News*, April 1, 2002.

Griffith, David. "*Hay Trabajo:* Poultry Processing, Rural Industrialization, and the Latinization of Low-Wage Labor." In *Any Way You Cut It*, eds.

Donald D. Stull, Michael J. Broadway, and David Griffith. Lawrence: University Press of Kansas, 1995.

Hays, Sharon. *Flat Broke with Children: Women in the Age of Welfare Reform.* New York: Oxford University Press, 2004.

Hilgartner, Stephen, and Charles L. Bosk. "The Rise and Fall of Social Problems: A Public Arenas Model." *American Journal of Sociology* 94, no. 1 (1988): 53–78.

Hollingshead, August. *Elmtown's Youth.* New York: John Wiley and Sons, 1949.

Hout, Michael. "More Universalism and Less Structural Mobility: The American Occupational Structure in the 1980s." *American Journal of Sociology* 93, no. 5 (1988): 1358–1400.

Howley, Caitlin. "Purpose and Place: Schooling and Appalachian Residence." *Journal of Appalachian Studies* 12, no. 1 (2006): 58–78.

Hudson, Lisa, Sally Aquilino, and Gregory Kienzl. "Postsecondary Participation Rates by Sex and Race/Ethnicity 1974–2003." NCES Research Brief, Washington, D.C., 2005.

Human Rights Watch. "Incarceration and Race." New York, 2000, available at www.hrw.org/reports/2000/usa/Rcedrg00–01.htm.

Jamieson, Lynn. "Migration, Place, and Class: Youth in a Rural Area." *Sociological Review* 48 (2000): 203–23.

Jekielek, Susan, and Brett Brown, "The Transition to Adulthood: Characteristics of Young Adults Ages 18 to 24 in America." *Kids Count/PRB/Child Trends Report on Census 2000.* The Annie Casey Foundation, Population Reference Bureau, and Child Trends: May 2005, 1–33.

Jencks, Christopher, and David Riesman. *The Academic Revolution.* New York: Doubleday, 1968.

Jencks, Christopher, Marshall Smith, Henry Acland, Mary Jo Bane, David Cohen, Herbert Gintis, Barbara Heyns, and Stephan Michelson. *Inequality: A Reassessment of the Effect of Family and Schooling in America.* New York: Basic Books, 1972.

Jensen, Leif. "New Immigrant Settlements in Rural America: Problems,

Prospects, and Policies." *Reports on Rural America* 1, no. 3 (2006): 6–31.

Johnson, Kenneth M., and Daniel T. Lichter. "Natural Increase: A New Source of Population Growth in Emerging Hispanic Destinations." *Population and Development Review* 34 (2008): 327–46.

Kalish, Mildred Armstrong. *Little Heathens: Hard Times and High Spirits on an Iowa Farm during the Great Depression.* New York: Bantam Dell, 2007.

Kefalas, Maria J. *Working-Class Heroes: Protecting Home, Community, and Nation in a Chicago Neighborhood.* Berkeley: University of California Press, 2003.

Keillor, Garrison. *Leaving Home.* New York: Penguin, 1990.

Kemple, James J., and Cynthia J. Willner, "Career Academies: Long-Term Impacts on Labor Market Outcomes, Educational Attainment, and Transitions to Adulthood." New York: Manpower Development Research Corporation, 2008.

Kendell, Gary. "Methamphetamine Abuse in Iowa: A Report to the Legislature." Des Moines, IA: Governor's Office of Drug Control Policy, 2007.

Kotlowitz, Alex. "Our Town." *New York Times Magazine,* August 5, 2007.

Krishna, Dean. "Try to Imagine the Iowa of My Dreams." Letter to the editor, *New York Times,* February 11, 2005.

Labaree, David F. *How to Succeed in School without Really Learning: The Credentials Race in American Education.* New Haven, CT: Yale University Press, 1997.

Lamont, Michele. *Money, Morals, and Manners: The Culture of the French and American Upper-Middle Class.* Chicago: University of Chicago Press, 1992.

Land, Robert E., Andrea Sarzynski, and Mark Muro. *Mountain Megas: America's Newest Metropolitan Places and a Partnership to Help Them Prosper.* Washington, D.C.: Brookings Institution Press, 2008.

Lareau, Annette. *Unequal Childhoods: Class, Race, and Family Life.* Berkeley: University of California Press, 2003.

Layton, Lyndsey. "Palin Apologizes for 'Real America' Comments." *Washington Post,* October 22, 2008.

Leistriz, F. Larry, and Katherine Meyer. "Farm Crisis in the Midwest: Trends and Implication." In *Beyond Amber Waves of Grain: An Examination of Social and Economic Restructuring in the Heartland,* eds. Paul Lasley, F. Larry Leistriz, Linda Lobao, and Katherine Meyer. Boulder, CO: Westview Press, 1995.

Lewis, Sinclair. *Main Street.* New York: Signet Classics, Penguin, 1998.

Lichter, Daniel T., Diane K. McLaughlin, and Gretchen T. Cornwell. "Migration and the Loss of Human Resources in Rural America." In *Investing in People: The Human Capital Needs of Rural America,* eds. Lionel J. Beaulieu and David Mulkey. Boulder, CO: Westview Press, 1995.

Longworth, Richard. *Caught in the Middle: America's Heartland in the Age of Globalism.* New York: Bloomsbury, 2007.

Lynd, Robert S., and Helen Merrell Lynd. *Middletown: A Study in Modern American Culture.* Orlando, FL: Harcourt Brace, 1957.

MacLeod, Jay. *Ain't No Makin' It: Aspirations and Attainment in a Low-Income Neighborhood.* 3rd ed. Boulder, CO: Westview Press, 2008.

Maharidge, Dale. *Denison, Iowa: Searching for the Soul of America through the Secrets of a Midwest Town.* New York: Simon and Schuster, 2005.

Manka, Maria Surma. "Midwest Monday: Iowa Guv Talks Solar Power." August 11, 2008, available at http://mariaenergia.blogspot.com/2008/08/midwest-monday-iowa-guv-talks-solar.html.

Marion, S., D. Mirochnik, E. McCaul, and W. McIntire. "The Educational and Work Experiences of Rural Youth: A Contextual and Regional Analysis." Orono: Center for Research and Evaluation, University of Maine, 1991.

Markus, H., and P. Nurius. "Possible Selves." *American Psychologist* 41, no. 9 (1986): 954–69.

Massey, Doug, and Nancy Denton. *American Apartheid: Segregation and the Making of the American Underclass.* Cambridge, MA: Harvard University Press, 1998.

McCaul, Edward. "Rural Public School Dropouts: Findings from High School and Beyond." *Journal of Research in Rural Education* 6, no. 1 (1989): 19–24.

McGranahan, David A. "Rural Workers at a Disadvantage in Job Opportunities." *Rural Development Perspectives* 4 (1988): 7–12.

McGranahan, David A., and Timothy R. Wojan. "The Creative Class: A Key to Rural Growth." *Amber Waves* (2007): 17–21.

————. "Recasting the Creative Class to Examine Growth Processes in Rural and Urban Counties." *Regional Studies* 41, no. 2 (2007): 197–216.

Meyer, John W. "Types of Explanation in the Sociology of Education." In *Handbook of Theory and Research for the Sociology of Education,* ed. John G. Richardson. New York: Greenwood, 1986.

Milner, Murray. *Freaks, Geeks and Cool Kids: American Teenagers and the Culture of Consumption.* New York: Routledge, 2004.

Mortimer, Jeylan. *Working and Growing Up in America.* Cambridge, MA: Harvard University Press, 2003.

Murray, Charles. *Real Education: Four Simple Truths for Bringing America's Schools Back to Reality.* New York: Crown Forum, 2008.

National Priorities Project. *Military Recruiting 2006.* Northampton, MA, 2008. http://www.nationalpriorities.org/Publications/Military-Recruiting-2006.html.

New Iowans Pilot Project. "Recruiting New Iowans into Model Communities." Des Moines, 2001. www.readiowa.org/finalreports2001/new iowanspilot.html.

Newman, Katherine. *Rampage: The Social Roots of School Shootings.* New York: Basic Books, 2004.

O'Hare, William P. "The Rise of Poverty in Rural America." Washington, D.C.: Population Reference Bureau, 15 (1980, ED 302 350).

Osgood, D. Wayne, Gretchen Ruth, Jacquelynne Eccles, Janis Jacobs, and

Bonnie Barber. "Six Paths to Adulthood: Fast Starters, Parents without Careers, Educated Partners, Educated Singles, Working Singles, and Slow Starters." In *On the Frontier of Adulthood: Theory, Research and Public Policy,* eds. Richard A. Settersten Jr., Frank F. Furstenberg Jr., and Ruben G. Rumbaut. Chicago: University of Chicago Press, 2005.

Parisi, Domenico, and Daniel T. Lichter. "Hispanic Segregation in America's New Rural Boomtowns." *Population Research Bureau,* September 2007, 1–4.

Petroski, William. "Taxpayers' Costs Top $5 Million for May Raid at Postville." *Des Moines Register,* October 14, 2008, A1.

Pollard, Kevin, and William P. O'Hare. "Beyond High School: The Experience of Rural and Urban Youth in the 1980s." Staff working paper. Washington, D.C.: Population Reference Bureau (1990, ED 326 363).

Popper, Deborah, and Frank Popper. "The Buffalo Commons: Then and Now." *Focus* 43, no. 4 (Winter 1993): 17–21.

_____. "Great Plains: From Dust to Dust." *Planning,* December 1987, 12–18.

Preston, Julia. "Meatpacker Faces Charges of Violating Child Labor Laws." *New York Times,* September 9, 2008.

Pritchett, Wendell. *Robert Clifton Weaver and the American City: The Life and Times of an Urban Reformer.* Chicago: University of Chicago Press, 2008.

Rathge, Richard, and Paula Highman. "Population Change in the Great Plains: A History of Prolonged Decline." *Rural Development Perspectives* 13, no. 1 (1998): 19–26.

Reich, Robert. "Hillary and Barack, Afta Nafta." http://robertreich.blog spot.com/2008/02/hillary-and-barack-afta-nafta.html.

Ritter, John. "Towns Offer Free Land to Newcomers." *USA Today,* February 9, 2005, 1A.

Rogers, Heather. "Literary Amenities and Cultural Scenes: Assessing the Differential Impact of Quality and Spatial Concentration." Working paper. The Cultural Policy Center at the University of Chicago, 2004.

Rosenbaum, James. *Beyond College for All: Career Paths for the Forgotten Half.* New York: Russell Sage Foundation, 2004.

_____. *Making Inequality: The Hidden Curriculum of High School Tracking.* New York: John Wiley and Sons, 1976.

Rural Youth Suicide Prevention Workshop. "Preventing Youth Suicide in Rural America: Recommendations to States." State and Territorial Injury Prevention Director's Association, Atlanta, GA, and Suicide Prevention Resource Center, Newton, MA, 2008. www.stipda.org and www.sprc.org.

Salamon, Sonya. *Newcomers to Old Towns: Suburbanization of the Heartland.* Chicago: University of Chicago Press, 2003.

Schmidt, William. "Ups and Downs Aside, Iowa Has Middleness." *New York Times,* February 7, 1988.

Settersten, Richard A. Jr., Frank F. Furstenberg Jr., and Ruben G. Rumbaut. *On the Frontier of Adulthood: Theory, Research and Public Policy.* Chicago: University of Chicago Press, 2005.

Sherwood, R. A. "A Conceptual Framework for the Study of Aspirations." In R. Quaglia, ed., *Research in Rural Education,* 6, no. 2 (1989): 61–66.

Shipler, David K. *The Working Poor: Invisible in America.* New York: Knopf, 2004.

Sirota, David. "Hillary Clinton's NAFTA U-Turn Says Something about Her—and Us." *Seattle Times,* February 25, 2008.

Snyder, Anastasia, R. "Teen Pregnancy, Rural Poverty, and Youth Well-Being Outcomes." November 28, 2007, available at http://www.author stream.com/Presentation/Funtoon-31047-Teen-Pregnancy-Rural-Poverty-Youth-Outcomes-Objectives-Todays-Talk-Measuring-Disc-and-as-Entertainment-ppt-powerpoint.

Snyder, Anastasia R., Susan L. Brown, and Erin P. Condo. "Residential Differences in Family Formation: The Significance of Cohabitation." *Rural Sociology* 69, no. 2 (2004): 235–60.

Stauber, Karl. "Why Invest in Rural America—and How? A Critical Public Policy Question for the 21st Century." In *Exploring Policy Options for a New Rural America.* Kansas City, MO: Federal Reserve Bank of Kansas City, Center for the Study of Rural America, 2001.

Stepp, Laura. *Unhooked: How Young Women Pursue Sex, Delay Love, and Lose at Both.* New York: Riverhead Books, 2007.

Stevens, Mitchell. *Creating a Class: College Admissions and the Education of Elites.* Cambridge, MA: Harvard University Press, 2007.

Stevens, Mitchell L., Elizabeth A. Armstrong, and Richard Arum. "Sieve, Incubator, Temple, Hub: Empirical and Theoretical Advances in the Sociology of Higher Education." *Annual Review of Sociology* 34 (2008): 127–51.

Stull, Donald D., Michael J. Broadway, and David Griffith, eds. *Any Way You Cut It: Meat Processing and Small-Town America.* Lawrence: University Press of Kansas, 1995.

Tankersley, Jim, and Christi Parsons. "Immigration Roils Small-Town America." *Swamp,* September 25, 2008.

Tolbert, Charles M., Michael D. Irwin, Thomas A. Lyson, and Albert R. Nucci. "Civic Community in Small-Town America: How Civic Welfare Is Influenced by Local Capitalism and Civic Engagement." *Rural Sociology* 67, no. 1 (2002): 90–113.

Understanding Rural America. Washington, D.C.: Agricultural Information Bulletin, no. 710, February 1995.

United States Census Bureau. *The 2009 Statistical Abstract.* Washington, D.C.: Census Bureau, 2009.

United States Department of Agriculture. "Measuring Rurality: What Is Rural?" Washington, D.C.: Economic Research Service, USDA, 2008.

———. "Rural Income, Poverty and Welfare: Rural Poverty." Washington, D.C.: Economic Research Service, USDA, 2004.

Vanden Brook, Tom. "Bonuses Boost Reservist's Recruitment." *USA Today,* March 27, 2008.

Walberg, H.J. "Student Aspirations: National and International Perspectives." *Research in Rural Education* 6, no. 2 (1989): 1–9.

Weiland, Matt, and Sean Wilsey, eds. *State By State: A Panoramic Portrait of America.* New York: HarperCollins, 2008.

Williams, Florence. "Frank and Deborah Popper's 'Buffalo Commons' Is Creeping toward Reality." *Plains Sense-High Country News,* January 15, 2001.

Willis, Paul. *Learning to Labour: How Working-Class Kids Get Working-Class Jobs.* London: Saxon House, 1981.

Wilson, William Julius. *The Truly Disadvantaged: The Inner City, the Underclass, and Public Policy.* Chicago: University of Chicago Press, 1987.

Wojan, Timothy R., and David A. McGranahan. "Ambient Returns: Creative Capital's Contribution to Local Manufacturing Competitiveness." *Agricultural and Resource Economics Review* 36, no. 1 (2007): 133–48.

Wolfe, Thomas. *I Am Charlotte Simmons: A Novel.* New York: Farrar, Strauss, and Giroux, 2004.

Wright, Evan. *Generation Kill: Devil Dogs, Iceman, Captain America, and the New Face of American War.* New York: Putnam, 2004.

Index

223